THE U.S.-MEXICAN BORDER IN THE TWENTIETH CENTURY

THE U.S.-MEXICAN BORDER IN THE TWENTIETH CENTURY

A HISTORY OF ECONOMIC AND SOCIAL TRANSFORMATION

DAVID E. LOREY

A Scholarly Resources Inc. Imprint
Wilmington, Delaware

Scholarly Resources Inc.
104 Greenhill Avenue
Wilmington, DE 19805-1897
www.scholarly.com

Library of Congress Cataloging-in-Publication Data

Lorey, David E.
   The U.S.-Mexican border in the twentieth century / David E. Lorey.
     p.   cm.   (Latin American silhouettes)
   Includes bibliographical references (p.   ) and index.
   ISBN 0-8420-2756-4 (paper : alk. paper). —ISBN 0-8420-2755-6
(cloth : alk. paper)
   1. Mexican-American Border Region—History—20th century.
2. United States—Relations—Mexico. 3. Mexico—Relations—United
States.   I. Title.   II. Title: United States-Mexican border in the
twentieth century.   III. Series.
F787.L67   1999
972'.1—dc21   99-12906
                                     CIP

In memory of my father,
Emmett Lorey (1928–1998),
whose immigration to California after the war
was one of the millions that shaped
the contemporary border

ABOUT
THE AUTHOR

DAVID E. LOREY received his B.A. in history from Wesleyan University and his M.A. and Ph.D. in Latin American history from the University of California, Los Angeles (UCLA). From 1989 to 1997 he was coordinator of the Program on Mexico and visiting professor of history at UCLA. He also has taught Latin American history at Pomona College, the University of Southern California, and the Universidad de las Américas in Puebla, Mexico.

Since July 1997, Professor Lorey has served as program officer for Latin America at the William and Flora Hewlett Foundation in Menlo Park, California. His publications include *The University System and Economic Development in Mexico since 1929* (1993); *The Rise of the Professions in Mexico* (1994); *United States-Mexico Border Statistics since 1900* (1990); and *United States-Mexico Border Statistics since 1900: 1990 Update* (1993).

CONTENTS

Preface • ix

INTRODUCTION **DEFINING THE REGION, OBJECTIVES,
AND APPROACHES** 1

CHAPTER ONE **DISTINGUISHING CHARACTERISTICS AND EARLY HISTORY:
FRONTIER, BORDERLANDS, BORDER REGION** 15

The Colonial Period: Life on a New World Frontier • 17
From Frontier to Borderlands • 23
Conflict between the United States and Mexico • 28
Early Border Phenomena • 30

CHAPTER TWO **BOOMS AND BUSTS ON THE BORDER:
ECONOMIC DEVELOPMENT, 1880s TO 1920s** 35

The First Border Boom, 1880 to 1910 • 35
The Border Economy during the Mexican Revolution • 40
Prohibition on the Border • 45
Early Free Trade • 49

CHAPTER THREE   **LIFE ON THE BORDER:
                SOCIAL CHANGE, 1880s TO 1930s**   53

                1880s to 1910 • 53
                Causes of the Mexican Revolution • 56
                The Social Character of the Revolution
                    in the Mexican North • 63
                The Revolutionary Period on the U.S. Side
                    of the Border • 66
                Transboundary Population Movements during Revolution,
                    Prohibition, and Depression • 69

CHAPTER FOUR   **BOOMS AND BUSTS ON THE BORDER,
                1930s AND 1940s**   77

                The Great Depression • 78
                World War II • 82

CHAPTER FIVE   **ECONOMIC TRENDS SINCE 1950:
                LEGACIES OF THE WARTIME ECONOMY**   93

                The Border Economy Comes of Age • 94
                Mexican Government Policy and the Border:
                    PRONAF and BIP—the *Maquiladoras* • 103

CHAPTER SIX   **THE CONSEQUENCES OF RAPID GROWTH
                IN THE BORDER REGION:
                SOCIAL AND CULTURAL CHANGE SINCE THE 1940s**   117

                Population and Migration • 118
                Urbanization • 124
                Mexican Americans • 134
                The Impact of Migration on Sending Communities • 137
                Cultural Evolutions • 139

CHAPTER SEVEN   **U.S.-MEXICAN RELATIONS AT THE BORDER:
                1890s TO 1990s**   153

                The Elusive Boundary: Water, Environmental Issues,
                    and Drug Trafficking • 154
                Migration • 162
                NAFTA in the Border Region • 169

                Suggested Readings • 183
                Index • 189

PREFACE

This book had its genesis in a course that I taught on border history at UCLA in 1996 and 1997. When I complained to Richard Hopper, general manager at Scholarly Resources, that no basic text on the history of the U.S.-Mexican border existed, he suggested that I turn my lecture notes into just such a book. Without fully appreciating all that the conversion would entail, I agreed. A year after I last taught the course, the work was finally completed.

This volume, like the course, draws largely upon the work of others. I owe a major debt to the historians who have chosen the border as their territory. As a field of study, the border is not a forgiving master. Primary sources and the secondary literature are difficult to access. The physical terrain lacks many comforts. The border region is still a geographic discipline too often relegated to second-rank courses and career tracks. And promotion and tenure are often less secure for border scholars than they are for other academics.

Of the brave historians who have taken on the border, the group involved in the National Endowment for the Humanities-funded Borderlands Atlas project at UCLA (of which I was a late inductee) has earned my greatest appreciation. I have relied extensively on their work and that of Norris Hundley (the project's organizer). I have also borrowed from the published and unpublished work of many other border historians. In the text, notes, and suggested readings, I have attempted to acknowledge their contributions. Chapter notes are limited to the most essential references; a more ponderous scholarly apparatus would be of little use to the student or general reader and would be superfluous for the expert already familiar with the literature. I hope that I have slighted no one by omission or misrepresentation. All errors of fact or interpretation are, of course, mine.

From the outset I conceived of my contribution to this project as a synthesis, highlighting the common themes that run through border historiography and focusing on the big picture. Thus, I have organized my review of recent border research around what I see as the central issues in the evolution of the region: boom-and-bust cycles; federal subsidization of border-region economic development; the resourcefulness of border peoples, past and present; and the richness of border culture.

During the course of the project, I incurred many specific debts. An inner circle of border historians—in particular, Paul Ganster and Oscar Martínez, both of whom read the entire manuscript—provided constant support, generously sharing their research and improving my work with their detailed criticism. Bill Beezley guided me dependably and well in this as in other joint ventures. Both Enrique Ochoa and my father repeatedly inquired about the book's progress, reminding me not to let up. My colleagues at the William and Flora Hewlett Foundation, where I currently serve as program officer for Latin America, provided a high-energy intellectual environment and the challenging perspectives of their several disciplines. Mariana Alvarado offered crucial, last-minute bibliographical support. And Rick Hopper at Scholarly Resources gave me the timely encouragement I needed to keep me going.

D.E.L.
Menlo Park, California

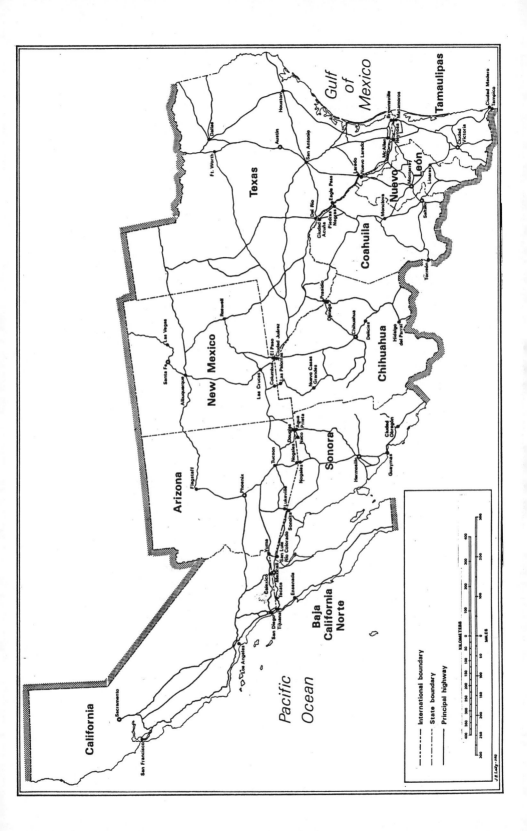

INTRODUCTION | # DEFINING THE REGION, OBJECTIVES, AND APPROACHES

THE 2,000-MILE-LONG international boundary between the United States and Mexico gives shape to a unique economic, social, and cultural entity. The U.S.-Mexican border region has the distinction of being the only place in the world where a highly developed country and a developing nation meet and interact. The complex history of the economy and society of the border in the twentieth century makes the region a fascinating area to study.

At the end of the nineteenth century the U.S.-Mexican border region was a vaguely defined territory in which sparse populations, separated by an international boundary, came into uncertain contact. With a few exceptions, the border neither attracted much notice nor caused much alarm. Undefined for most of its length, the boundary presented little inconvenience to residents of the states that abutted it. A century later, however, the 2,000-mile demarcating line defines a region in which "two different civilizations face each other and overlap."[1] During a century of rapid and dramatic change in both the United States and Mexico, the border has come to unite as well as divide the two countries and their historical experiences. By the 1990s the boundary was, paradoxically, both more and less intrusive than it had been at the beginning of the century.

The border region emerged over the course of the twentieth century as a place of pressing concern for local, regional, and national leaders. In particular, after the United States and Mexico implemented a free-trade pact in 1994 to confront the economic blocs of Europe and the Far East, the area became a central stage in the international politico-economic theater. Integration, which has tended to express itself most dramatically along the international boundary, brings with it a wide array of economic, social, and political challenges for border residents, scholars and students, and policymakers.

The border region is characterized by a binational economy of astounding complexity. It has seen rapid transformation in a short span of time, changing from a cattle ranching and mining area that attracted U.S. and European capitalists in the late nineteenth century to the center of a lucrative vice- and pleasure-based tourist industry, to a region that, after World War II, attracted an extraordinary amount of international capital to its manufacturing and services sector. To complicate matters further, the border economy has always been characterized by convulsive booms and busts.

After World War II the U.S. border states emerged as international leaders in aircraft, defense-related, and high-tech innovations. On the Mexican side of the boundary, assembly plants, generally known as *maquilas* or *maquiladoras* and established beginning in the mid-1960s, accounted for as much as 40 percent of Mexico's manufactured exports by the mid-1990s. In several subregions along the international boundary, the border economy is the *only* economy. As people crossing from Tijuana to San Diego spend an annual 1 billion dollars in retail and service sectors, trade officials representing the two cities team up to invite worldwide productive facilities to their international, twin-city site.

The border region, also socially complex, is characterized by a tremendous movement of people, both short term and permanent, both within and between Mexico and the United States. It is instructive to note that, of all persons who cross the border from the South to the North, only 1 percent do so illegally.[2] Ironically, this small population frequently constitutes the only border story deemed worth reporting by the mass media of both countries. In contrast to the dozens or hundreds who may cross illegally every night, some 40,000 people travel from Tijuana to San Diego to work every day. Each year the border sees 250 million legal crossings each way, mostly Mexican shoppers who spend an estimated 25 billion dollars in the United States and pay 2 billion dollars in sales taxes without receiving any public services. The large numbers of people who live on both sides of the border, who move back and forth legally, and who constitute the great majority of border residents are the primary focus of this study.

The border society that has emerged over time as a result of massive population relocations is distinct from that of either the United States or Mexico; it is both an amalgam of the two and something entirely different from either. The border's social matrix is perhaps best perceived in its cities, large and small, that dot the landscape of the region. Ciudad Juárez is the sixth largest urban conglomeration in Mexico; Tijuana is the eighth largest. Ciudad Juárez-El Paso (or Paso del Norte), considered by some to be the border's unofficial capital, is a metropolitan area with a population between 1.5 and 2 million divided into two moieties by the international boundary. In towns all along the border, binational Rotary Clubs meet weekly, alternating countries. Calexico and Mexicali cooperate on fire fighting and providing emergency medical services; El Paso and Ciudad Juárez cooperate on policing the drug trade.

The culture of contemporary border peoples is extraordinarily rich. Originally inhabited by a great diversity of indigenous populations, the area was later populated by Europeans, people of African origin, Native American migrants from central Mexico, Asians, and persons of mixed ethnicity. The culture that developed from the experience of these various border peoples (and the progeny resulting from their interaction in the region) is unique. The international boundary is a place where the English and Spanish languages are increasingly blended, where bilingualism flourishes, where multiculturalism is a fact of daily life.

The border disappears into the Pacific Ocean.
Paul Ganster, Institute for Regional Studies of the Californias

The region hosts a dizzying array of transborder cultural phenomena: televisions and radio stations, whether broadcasting in English or Spanish, draw advertising revenue from businesses on both sides of the border; flags are raised on both sides on September 16, Mexico's Independence Day; and, on Thanksgiving Day, relatives travel from the U.S. side to eat turkey dinners with their families across the boundary. Border phenomena have spread farther than most people realize: Mexican-style salsa, for example, has replaced ketchup as the most popular table condiment in the United States; Corona beer has become the leading imported brew in the United States (ahead of Heineken); and Mexican piñatas are ritually demolished at children's birthday parties throughout North America.

Perhaps at least partly because of this great diversity and complexity, many myths about the region exist and mythmaking continues. Often U.S. citizens, even those who live in the border region, perceive the area in terms of undocumented migration, drug trafficking, and decaying cities. Some feel they have lost control of "their" border. One observer summarizes the popular images as follows: "The border is drowning in the filth of a putrescent Rio Grande aglow with toxic wastes; it is terminally ill with the rampant pox of poverty known as *colonias* [illegal and irregular settlements on the U.S. side of the border]; it is a land of social injustice where evil foreign *maquiladoras* unmercifully exploit downtrodden workers for their cheap labor; swarms of huddling illegals poise nightly to pour northward across the border to overwhelm American social services and steal jobs from honest workers while free-loading on the largess of hard-pressed American taxpayers."[3]

Frequently accompanying such conceptions are stereotyped, monochromatic characterizations of Mexicans, Texans, Californians, and border society in general. During the North American Free Trade Agreement (NAFTA) debate in 1992, presidential candidate Ross Perot summed up the perceptions of many observers when he portrayed the border region as "one large slum." The area, with its long history of vice-based tourism, continues to be seen as a den of sin and iniquity, catering to prostitution, drinking, corruption, drugs, and gambling for both Mexicans and U.S. citizens. More recently, the border has come to be closely identified with its economic boom; the *maquiladora* assembly plants have taken the place of casinos and brothels in the litany of abuses allegedly perpetrated upon border people. Some observers have come to see the larger boundary-development model—relocation of production in line with global trends, freer trade—as a model of all that can go wrong in the new global economy.

Without denying poverty, corruption, drugs, decay, pollution, or unequal distribution of wealth, this study endeavors to demonstrate that such characterizations of the region obscure more than they reveal. Recognizing that there is some basis for the images that predominate in public discourse about the border, this volume explores the complex causes and consequences of such phenomena. The reality is far more interesting than popular myths and stereotypes suggest.

Part of the challenge of studying the border region stems from the difficulty of defining the scope of the geographical and temporal area to be covered. Where and what is the U.S.-Mexican border region? Why does it merit attention as a separate entity? In contrast to most regions, its defining boundary runs *through* it rather than around it. And that boundary was not determined by geography; it was invented by two warring nation-states, which established it a century and a half ago in a region that neither ever completely dominated. It is administered today by outsiders in distant Mexico City and Washington, DC.

The border region can be defined in two basic ways. From the Mexican viewpoint it is that area of the Spanish and Mexican far-northern frontier where Europeans and Mexicans of mixed ethnicity encountered and settled among indigenous Americans, a region stretching from the Gulf of Mexico to the Pacific Ocean. From the U.S. perspective it is the contiguous section of the continent acquired by the United States, beginning with the Louisiana Purchase in 1803; continuing with the acquisition of Texas, the Oregon Territory, and the Mexican cession of 1848; and ending with the 1853 Gadsden Purchase of the lands between the Gila River and the present Mexican boundary. With much justice the region is sometimes called MexAmerica. The moniker is appealing because it is accurate: the border region is perhaps best defined in general terms as the area—economic, social, and cultural—where Mexico and the United States have overlapped and interacted for the last 150 years.

A border marker east of San Diego is shown here.
The border remains informally marked and unguarded over most of its length.
David E. Lorey

Because of the vague limits of the territory and the shifting boundary, I define the region, when necessary, using the simple, if anachronistic, concept of states. The statistical data in the following chapters generally refer to the ten border states in the United States and Mexico: California, Arizona, New Mexico, and Texas; and Baja California, Sonora, Chihuahua, Coahuila, Nuevo León, and Tamaulipas.* The area included in this definition—960,000 square miles—is considerably larger than Western Europe.

It is also necessary to make a temporal division. Drawing on the long and complex history of the region, I make the following chronological distinctions: (1) a frontier period, or a period of multiple, interpenetrating frontiers, lasting from contact between Europeans and Native Americans to the end of the colonial years; (2) a borderlands era from 1803 through Mexican independence in 1821 to the end of the U.S.-Mexican war in 1848; and (3) the years since 1848, for which a distinct U.S.-Mexican border region can be clearly identified. This third period is divided into two parts: 1848 to the 1880s (after which the railroad linked the area to world markets for border products), and the 1880s to the 1990s (from the first major economic boom along the boundary to the regulated integration provided by NAFTA a century later). This study focuses on the last stretch, from the 1880s to the time of publication. Chapter 2 briefly reviews the previous epochs.[4]

In both geographical and temporal terms, however, the definition of the region must remain flexible. Economic, social, political, and cultural borders fall in different places; there are subregions of the border world that relate only loosely to state boundaries. For example, border phenomena are experienced as far from the international boundary as the cities of Chicago and New York and as far as the states of Washington, Oregon, and Colorado in the United States and Sinaloa, Durango, Jalisco, and the Yucatán peninsula in Mexico, where *maquiladora* production has pulled people into the

---

*Unless otherwise noted, data for the period from 1900 to the 1990s are from David Lorey, *U.S.-Mexican Border Statistics since 1900* (Los Angeles: UCLA Latin American Center Publications, 1990), and David Lorey, *U.S.-Mexican Border Statistics since 1900: 1990 Update* (Los Angeles: UCLA Latin American Center Publications, 1993). Data for earlier periods are drawn from the sources cited in the chapter notes and from those listed in Suggested Readings at the end of the volume.

border world.[5] The long-term trend is a region that continues to grow socially, culturally, and psychologically. Social networks are created and cultural patterns established that constantly shift the boundaries of the border world outward. This book does not attempt to force the history of the border region to conform to what have become the standard periodizations for U.S. and Mexican history, for it does not easily fall into these divisions. Instead, the focus on major economic and social currents in border history brings to light unusual and sometimes overlapping time frames.

In the region so defined there is much to study that is unique to it and directly attributable to the existence of the international boundary. The economies of the region and its inhabitants share a common history of boom-and-bust cycles, migration within and between nation-states, and intense sociocultural blending and assimilation. In the sense that border phenomena are increasingly prevalent and increasingly shared, these aspects of the area, which are endlessly fascinating to scholars and students, become more and more relevant to all of us who live in North America.

A major challenge in writing a primer on the modern border is the legacy of past treatments of the area. Until recently, historians have not focused on the unique characteristics of the U.S.-Mexican border region's evolution. Following a traditional, national approach, they have given separate treatment to the histories of the northern states of Mexico and the southwestern portion of the United States, or the U.S. West. Only during the last two decades of the twentieth century did the field of border history come into its own. Now, in addition to their own work in archives and local collections, historians of the international boundary are being influenced by the work of border scholars in a diverse array of natural and social sciences, as they uncover a wealth of new sources and approach them with new methodologies to shed light on the complex past and present of the transboundary area.

A certain quantity of ideological baggage also has shaped the field. Scholars and other observers have tended to view the border region alternately as a model for U.S.-Mexican economic integration, a model for U.S.-Mexican relations, and an example of all the negative aspects of unchecked economic growth and U.S.-Mexican interaction. Such normative judgments have colored their analyses. I suggest that the border be approached as a laboratory for the study of transboundary economic, social, and cultural phenomena in the new global economy. While the world economy has become more global in nature, it also has become more regional: the U.S.-Mexican boundary offers a unique window on this apparent paradox. To prejudge the trajectory or meaning of border history is to risk the loss of this valuable vantage point.

Drawing on the approaches and findings of recent historical research, this text focuses on social, economic, and cultural themes in the history of the border region from the last quarter of the nineteenth century to the 1990s. Despite the importance of the ten border states to both the United States and Mexico, and for all the fascinating history of their interaction, we know very little about the most pressing dimensions of life and livelihood along the international boundary throughout the twentieth century. *The U.S.-Mexican Border in the Twentieth Century*, therefore, has three basic objectives: First, it seeks to treat the area as historically coherent. The chapters that follow adopt a region-centered focus, emphasizing crossboundary society, culture, and economic ties. Second, the book surveys the historical evolution of the region with an eye to the relationship between social and economic change, seeking to understand, for example, how boom and bust shaped border society. Third, this study considers historical change in the region as much as possible from the inside—that is, from the perspective of people who lived through and prompted the changes.

The overall approach adopted here is somewhat unusual. Topics are discussed sometimes narratively and sometimes analytically. Multiple perspectives are emphasized in order to explore the complexity of the region's past. No single ideological approach is forced on the reader because no single approach can adequately explain the evolution of border reality, and no magic paradigm can unlock the mysteries of the border's past and present. Instead, I draw on and combine diverse perspectives in an effort to contribute to an understanding of the boundary area.

This study uses macro-level approaches to explore the way in which the evolution of the border region has been shaped by outside phenomena and trends. The discussion includes world economic cycles, which have greatly affected the area. It is also sometimes useful to consider the bor-

The Rio Grande at Ciudad Juárez-El Paso
is a "militarized" section of the border.
David E. Lorey

der as an extension of nation-states, to see it as a locus of struggles between nations, and to view regional conflict and border policy issues accordingly. At another extreme the book takes a micro-level approach to the exploration of border evolutions. The area has been characterized throughout its long history by an active and vibrant society that emerged despite the strong influence of external forces. Understanding local and subregional developments—particularly those that involve individuals and communities spanning the boundary—is as important as understanding external factors in explaining this history. Symbiotic and interdependent relationships in the region are also examined, in order to analyze the developing links between the two societies and economies. Interconnectedness is a major aspect in the area's development. In particular the historical experiences of border towns illustrate how local border societies and economies developed over time. Through this approach it becomes evident that the historical interplay of exogenous and endogenous forces has given shape to the U.S.-Mexican boundary region and its social realities.

It is important to clarify what a book is not in addition to what it is. This study does not emphasize political issues or consider the national policymaking processes of Mexico or the United States in any direct way. Although it surveys the experiences of Mexican-origin populations in the border region, it is intended as neither a book about Mexican-origin peoples in the United States nor a study of documented or undocumented migration. This is not a book about NAFTA or U.S.-Mexican relations at the strategic level, and it does not pretend to present histories of either the United States or Mexico more broadly during the period at hand. Each of these topics, though treated in the chapters that follow, is considered in the context of questions of major historical significance for the evolution of the U.S.-Mexican border region.

Perhaps the most general goal of this book is to advance the notion that the pressing issues facing North America must be addressed in a new regional context, a context that includes Mexico, the United States, and the boundary area that unites them. With their destinies now explicitly linked under NAFTA, the United States and Mexico will certainly face problems that the border region has struggled with since its creation. The fundamental challenge for the North American community is to develop multilateral and collaborative solutions to common difficulties; in fact, the long-term objective of thinking (on a personal level) and policymaking (on a social level) should be to *overcome* the U.S.-Mexican border. An understanding of the border region is essential to an understanding of the current shape of North America, the problems it faces, and the best way to meet future challenges.

NOTES

1. Ross, *Views across the Border,* p. xii.
2. In 1996 only 1.1 percent of the U.S. population comprised illegal Mexican migrants; only 15 percent of the Mexican-origin population of the United States was in the country illegally. See Frank D. Bean et al., "The Quantification of Migration between Mexico and the United States" (binational study of migration between Mexico and the United States, July 1997), p. 61.
3. Timothy C. Brown, "The Fourth Member of NAFTA: The U.S.-Mexico Border," *Annals of the American Academy of Political and Social Science* 550 (March 1997):

107. For an example of the continuing media and popular fascination with negative images, see Robert D. Kaplan, "Travels into America's Future," *Atlantic Monthly* 282:2 (July 1998): 47–68.

4. See Ellwyn R. Stoddard, "Frontiers, Borders, and Border Segmentation: Toward a Conceptual Clarification," *Journal of Borderlands Studies* 6:1 (Spring 1990): 1–22.

5. The areas experiencing the fastest growth in Mexican-origin population between 1990 and 1996 were the nonborder states of Oregon (55 percent), Nevada (77 percent), Nebraska (70 percent), Iowa (52 percent), Arkansas (104 percent), Tennessee (58 percent), Georgia (70 percent), North Carolina (73 percent), and Vermont (55 percent); Edwin Garcia and Ben Stocking, "Latinos on the Move to a New Promised Land," *San Jose Mercury News,* August 16, 1998.

CHAPTER ONE | # DISTINGUISHING CHARACTERISTICS AND EARLY HISTORY

FRONTIER, BORDERLANDS, BORDER REGION

THREE GEOGRAPHICAL FACTORS have shaped the border region from the time of earliest human settlement, through its period as frontier and borderlands, to the present. First, the region is vast in size. The area through which the international boundary passes is as large as Europe, stretching across North America from the Pacific Coast to the Gulf of Mexico and from the southern Rocky Mountains to the beginning of Mexico's Central Plateau.

Second, the region is mountainous, crisscrossed by a maze of inhospitable ranges that divide the area into isolated subregions. From Arizona southward the Sierra Madre Occidental—one hundred miles wide and twelve hundred miles long—cuts off the Central Plateau from the Pacific Coast. Along the eastern edge of the plateau the Sierra Madre separates the coast from the central regions for nearly one thousand miles. From west Texas to California high mountain ranges alternate with extensive basins. In an area this size and this mountainous, transportation and communication present major challenges. To date only two paved roads pierce the Mexican Sierra Madre Occidental from the interior to the coast.

Third, and perhaps most important, the border region is unremittingly arid: rainfall is inadequate for agriculture; it is also unpredictable—sporadic and occasionally destructive. Aridity has "indelibly stamped [border] society, affecting architecture, diet, attire, leisure, socialization, and travel."[1] Although the introduction of railroads, highways, and air travel improved accessibility to this vast and rugged terrain, the lack of both water and dependable rainfall remain major obstacles to human settlement throughout the area. Only at great federal expense was it possible to cross this geographical hurdle to create the U.S. West's stupendous late twentieth-century wealth in agriculture and industry. The development of the Mexican border states was also undergirded by successful control of the arid environment.

The region now encompassing the U.S.-Mexican border has a human history that stretches back approximately 12,000 years. The Americas in 1492 are estimated to have had a population of about sixty million; twenty-one million, or 35 percent, of this total are thought to have lived in Mexico. The area that today comprises the six Mexican and four U.S. border states was home to approximately one million people at the end of the fifteenth century. The aridity and ruggedness of much of the terrain meant that, in contrast to the inhabitants of central Mexico, most of the people of the region were nomadic hunters and gatherers, following a way of life that supported only relatively small populations. With one or two possible exceptions, the area did not generate major state organizations. Instead, it was characterized by small, autonomous, local communities economically and politically independent of one another.[2]

The culture of this aboriginal population was extremely heterogeneous. European settlers identified and named at least forty-five different groups. In the area of modern Chihuahua and Sonora, for example, there were six major languages: Tarahumara, Concho, Opata, Pima, Cahita, and Seri, each of which had several mutually unintelligible dialects. In New Mexico and Arizona, Spaniards identified at least fourteen distinct languages. In addition to ancient inhabitants there were Athabaskan groups, which had crossed the Rocky Mountains to settle their own frontier in more recent times: the Kiowa-Apache in central-western Texas; the Lipan-Apache in southwestern Texas; and the Jicarilla, Mescalero, Tonto Apache, and Navajo in parts of present-day Arizona, New Mexico, Sonora, and Chihuahua.

The majority of the inhabitants in the region were what early Spanish explorers termed *ranchería* people, those who lived in small hamlets with populations of only a few hundred each. Such settlements, often scattered over large surrounding territories, relied on wild foods as much as on planted crops. Where favorable agricultural conditions permitted, larger villages and more densely settled subregions existed. Along the banks of Sonora's important rivers, for example, relatively abundant supplies of water supported the villages of the Yaqui and Mayo. From 300 B.C. to 500 A.D., agriculturists cultivated maize, beans, and squash in the Salt and Gila River valleys in what is today Arizona. In northern Arizona and New Mexico the ancestors of the present Hopi people and the Tanoan Puebloans of the Rio Grande Valley created complex societies. Along the Rio Grande an estimated 40,000 people, practicing intensive agriculture, lived in highly organized villages.

These people's lives would be radically altered by contact with Europeans. Resistance to the changes introduced by outsiders through the centuries was substantial. Remarkably, three-quarters of the indigenous groups would survive to maintain some portion of their identities. This staying power resulted in a border society that is not simply a European transplant. In the 1960s twenty-five indigenous groups with distinct cultures, although greatly reduced in numbers, survived throughout the border region. These peoples represented more than one-half of the groups found in the area in the early 1500s.

THE COLONIAL PERIOD: LIFE ON
A NEW WORLD FRONTIER

The inhabitants of central Mexico—both natives and European settlers—perceived many obstacles to settling the Far North. Both the geographical landscape and the social setting made the area unattractive. Mountains and desert wastes combined with hostile indigenous populations to keep central Mexicans at bay for hundreds of years.

The region was termed the Gran Chichimeca, a land of barbarous peoples. Desultory exploration by Spaniards turned up little to justify settlement. Moving north along the coastlines, explorers surveyed unknown areas in search of cultures matching the civilization of central Mexico. In the five decades after Columbus the Spanish made a series of expeditions: Juan Ponce de León's 1513 expedition to Florida; Alonso Alvarez de Pineda's 1519 voyage around the Gulf of Mexico; Estevão de Gomes's 1524–25 *recorrido* (trip) up the northeast seaboard; Pedro de Quejo's 1525 voyage from Española to Delaware; Hernando de Soto's 1539–1543 visit to what is today Florida and the Atlantic Southeast; and João Rodrigues Cabrilho's 1542–43 expedition along the California coast. Although these initial *recorridos* by sea did not turn up much in the way of liquid wealth or concentrated, sedentary populations, subsequent myths of fabulous cities and Aztec-like civilizations fueled further exploration by land.

To the continued disappointment of explorers, land expeditions likewise discovered little to sustain the attention of European settlers. Alvar Núñez Cabeza de Vaca, who had been shipwrecked in Florida and wandered through the South as far west as Texas in 1528–1536, met many Native Americans, exchanged goods, and heard tales of the golden cities of Cíbola. He retold the stories to believing ears, including those of the Spanish viceroy. In 1540–1542, Francisco Vásquez de Coronado mounted a search for Cíbola, moving as far north as the modern-day state of Kansas. As the first large and carefully prepared Spanish expedition into the frontier, the *entrada* (entry) of Vásquez de Coronado contributed greatly to the cultural map of the aboriginal frontier. But explorers found no cities of fabulous wealth or any other compelling reason to settle the area.

The discovery of major veins of silver proved to be the stimulus for northern expansion during the colonial period. Mining became the motor of change throughout Mexico's Far North. Mining spurred migration and led to the development of a vibrant internal economy. Silver was discovered near Zacatecas in 1546 and at Guanajuato in 1550. In the following years, prospectors struck silver in San Luis Potosí, Pachuca, and Parral. The discovery of precious ore in the North resulted in a steady influx of settlers from central Mexico. As the silver boom continued, both Europeans and Native Americans moved north. The location of mining towns was a result of serendipity rather than planning. Because silver often was found in areas where other resources were lacking, mining towns developed complex social structures to meet the need for water, food, and fuel. The industry required large supplies of labor, wood, chemicals, staple foods, work animals, meat, iron, cloth, and leather. Large estates and smaller farms emerged to provision the mines; long-distance and local commerce developed to supply goods and credit. Along the major North-South road and its branch roads, thousands of mules carried commodities to the North and silver to the South.

A good example of this process of consolidation was the district of Nueva Vizcaya (now Chihuahua and Durango states). When silver was discovered in Parral in 1629, it quickly became one of the most important new settlements of the region, growing to three hundred families by 1632 and to eight hundred by 1640. The town not only produced wealth for those directly involved in the mining industry but also stimulated commerce, agriculture, and livestock raising in the surrounding region. By 1768, 149 occupations existed in the Parral region: although 40 percent of the population consisted of workers directly connected with mining, 10 percent of the population consisted of merchants and 33 percent consisted of artisans, including shoemakers, blacksmiths, tailors, and barbers. The town had one teacher and one surgeon.

The agricultural units that supported mining in the North ranged from small, intensive, irrigated plots near urban and mining centers, to small, family-owned farms and ranches, to great estates that often included many different properties managed as an integrated enterprise. The sixteenth century witnessed the rise of immense rural estates—haciendas—in some areas of the Far North as an outgrowth of mining operations. Miners, government officials, and military men acquired large holdings through land grants, purchase, and marriage. These units produced horses and mules, sheep for meat and wool, wheat, fruits and vegetables, oil, and wine. One of the largest estates in the eighteenth century was that of the Marques de Aguayo, which comprised fifteen million acres or about one-half the total land of Coahuila.[3] In many regions of the North the most common unit of agrarian production was the rancho. Throughout northern New Spain this small or medium holding of land was owned or leased by a family that also supplied most of the labor for the enterprise. In the most arid regions, livestock raising prevailed; in areas with precipitation or irrigation, crop and orchard production was common.

As other European powers became interested in the region and Spain's interest in protecting its empire grew, the Far North was increasingly the focus of attempts to impede intrusions. Defense against the spreading influence of the French, English, and Russians became one of the main foundations of settlement. The Spanish Crown and viceregal government in Mexico City devised several strategies to encourage settlement in the region. In order to pacify and populate the area at minimal cost, the Crown came to rely on two institutions with funds and personnel of its own: the military and the religious orders. This approach gave rise to the classic duo of European settlement in the North: the presidio and the mission. In an attempt to protect the silver trade, the viceregal government also organized armed convoys and established towns along the road from Mexico City to the mines.

The key to defense was the presidio, a walled enclosure with a church, a warehouse, and dwellings surrounded by grazing and agricultural lands. Presidial soldiers possessed the secrets of European technology and know-how; many of them worked as masons, carpenters, cowboys, ranchers, farmers, and artisans. Presidios often developed into permanent towns. Gradually, warfare against raiding natives gave way to campaigns by new settlers and the government to distribute food and supplies to the indigenous population.

Missions run by the regular orders (Franciscans and Jesuits) were expected to help pacify and incorporate Native Americans; they reduced into settled units the diverse and complex populations, particularly those that were semisedentary or nomadic. Missionaries introduced indigenous people to European ways of life. Within a century a string of missions stretched from the East to the West, across the frontier and up the Pacific Coast from Sinaloa to California.

Contrary to the classic conception of Spanish frontier society as mainly composed of missionaries and soldiers, civilian settlers were greater in number and contributed in more lasting ways to the region. Initially, civilian immigrants came from Spain and central Mexico; gradually, however, immigrants were drawn from adjacent provinces. Sinaloa supplied colonists for Sonora, and Sonora, in turn, supplied settlers for California. The nonindigenous working population grew rapidly and experienced some social mobility. Frontier towns attracted shopkeepers, notaries, craftsmen, artisans, and merchants, and rural areas soon had ranchers and truck gardeners who supplied the towns with staple goods.

Two characteristics made the frontier population unique. The inhabitants were of varied and mixed ethnicities, including Native Americans from all over the North and from central Mexico, as well as African Americans. Frontier society was also characterized by the prevalence of wage labor, which spread from the mines and urban settlements to agricultural areas, as a result of the high return on investment in the region, the need for skilled labor, and the location of the mining towns in areas of sparse indigenous populations.

Frontier populations transformed the indigenous societies with which they came into contact. Changes rippling outward in concentric circles from European settlements, particularly missions, reached the region before the Europeans did. In many areas, Spanish material culture, like metal goods and livestock, preceded the arrival of the Europeans. These introductions greatly disrupted the life-styles of indigenous groups. Intergroup raiding and warfare increased over the course of the eighteenth century.

The principal disruption was disease, introduced unintentionally by European settlers as they spread into the region. Although population decline on the frontier was not as great as it had been in central areas, the death toll from disease was nevertheless astounding. In the California missions, for example, Native American recruits generally survived mission life for ten years at most. In the region stretching from San Diego to San Francisco, the coastal indigenous population fell from 60,000 in 1769 to 35,000 in 1800, as the overall population of California fell from 300,000 in 1769 to 200,000 by the end of the colonial era in 1821. Within a century the native population of the frontier was cut to a little less than one-half of its precontact size.

Spaniards tried various overt ways of reshaping indigenous life. In and around the missions nonreligious impacts were probably more significant than religious impacts. Although legally closed to civilian settlers, the missions attracted people to adjacent areas. Because settlers demanded access to native labor, missions often developed into labor-recruitment institutions. They were surrounded by flourishing agricultural establishments and indigenous people who passed time among both nonreligious settlers and friars. In those mission areas that were near mines, population movement was particularly pronounced, and conflict between civilian employers and the mission fathers for control of natives was constant.

Because the Spaniards, who had come from urban environments, felt that city life was part of being civilized, they encouraged Native Americans to live in or near missions. Indigenous people were taught to husband European domestic animals—horses, sheep, goats, pigs, and chickens; cultivate European crops; use such iron tools as wheels, saws, chisels, planes, nails, and spikes; and practice those arts and crafts that Spaniards regarded as essential for civilization. Missionaries attempted to instill European ideas of discipline in several realms, and they introduced clocks and bells, thus imparting to the native population European notions of time.

The expansion of Europeans—missionaries, soldiers, landowners, merchants, workers—into the North did not take the form of a constantly advancing frontier. Nomadic natives of the region reacted fiercely against the occupation of their territory and the increased competition for its meager resources. Most threatening were raids of the Apaches and Comanches, displaced from their ancient homelands by French and British settlers from the North and East. The opening of the North during the second half of the sixteenth century produced fifty years of conflict known as the War of the Gran Chichimeca. Neither the strictly military approach nor the missions and the provision of food pacified the region. Native Americans who lived in close proximity to European settlers resisted the steady change to their lives in a number of other ways. They fled missions, organized local rebellions that addressed specific grievances, and engaged in some remarkably successful larger revolts.

Resistance and rebellion meant that by the mideighteenth century the Spanish settlers could claim to have made only limited inroads into the region. They were besieged by powerful and confident nomadic groups on horseback. Time and again revolts forced the Spaniards to retreat and abandon their positions. By 1700 it was clear that the northward expansion of New Spain had failed to reach the almost unlimited horizons of the early years. Practical frontiers had to be drawn, as the imperial emphasis shifted from northward expansion to defense and consolidation.

Throughout the long colonial period, frontier life, which took on processes and structures all its own, was increasingly characterized by a unique, defining culture. Settlers to the region modified Spanish customs, language, religion, and work habits in the new environment. Farming methods, labor, architecture, and local celebrations were all affected by changed circumstances. Isolation from the earlier settled regions of New Spain and from each other forced frontier dwellers to adapt to local conditions, often producing in them social and personal characteristics that differed markedly from those of the residents of central Mexico. A pride in the ability to overcome frontier challenges fostered a sense of distinction from the populations of other areas of Mexico.

FROM FRONTIER TO BORDERLANDS

During the relatively brief span from Mexican independence in 1821 to the end of the war between the United States and Mexico in 1848, Spain's far-northern frontier territories became borderlands—the relatively undefined and frequently contested terrains between Mexico and the United States. Many patterns and processes that first appeared during this twenty-seven-year period would shape border society for the following century. Mexico sought to integrate the area into the national mainstream by building political and economic ties. But attempts to make the region part of the nation fell short of success. The era culminated in the acquisition of a great portion of the Mexican North by the United States.

Following independence, the two key frontier institutions—the presidio and the mission—fell into irreversible decline. The presidio lost its imperial purpose, and resident soldiers focused their energies on non-defensive activities. The missions came under sharp attack from Mexican liberals, who denounced them for oppressing the native population, accumulating nonproductive wealth and property, and interfering in affairs of state. Local pressure to secularize the missions, which would turn them into parish churches and pueblos, fundamentally resulted from non-religious settlers' desire for land, however. By the mid-1830s, secularization was a fact in Texas, Arizona, California, and New Mexico.

Mexico's inability to integrate its northern frontier into the country's core reflected, above all, the difficulties of establishing political stability after independence. A complete collapse of effective administration in the North doomed the borderlands to remain on the periphery economically and politically. Although Mexicans understood the challenges of incorporating the region into national life, efforts to do so were overshadowed by the exigencies of nation building. Fewer than fifteen thousand Mexicans lived in the area, and frontier and central regions did not identify with one another. Independence encouraged a return to local autonomy rather than a strengthening of ties between the North and the center.

Several additional factors pulled central Mexico and the borderlands apart. In 1824 the first national constitution created a federal republic of states and territories in which states achieved considerable autonomy in decision making but territories came under the direct control of the Mexican Congress. Under the 1824 constitution, California and New Mexico were territories, but Congress never enacted regulations for their internal governance. Texans reacted bitterly to the loss of their voice when the Mexican constitution joined them to the more powerful and populous Coahuila as the state of Coahuila y Texas. In 1836, President Antonio López de Santa Anna introduced a new centralist constitution that converted the states into military departments, a status they would retain until 1847. The result of these actions in the North was a growing sense of separation from central authority. Relations between periphery and center became increasingly strained.

Another force that tended to move the North out of the central Mexican sphere of influence was commerce. Illegal trade with French, English,

and U.S. citizens had existed under Spain, but commerce with foreigners increased dramatically after the young nation officially authorized
such trade in 1821. The bulk of business was with the United States and
Europe rather than with central Mexico. American farm products and British
manufactured goods were exchanged for a variety of Mexican frontier products: hides from California; mules from New Mexico; and wheat, salt, silver, tallow, and other items from throughout the borderlands area. North
American and European merchants established themselves in ports and cities,
providing both capital and trade goods to the local population. These commercial links strengthened the economic independence of the North and
tied it ever more closely to the United States.

Border society underwent several important changes during the early
national period. The most notable was the decline in sedentary, native population and the increase in the numbers of Europeans and mestizos. Under
Mexican rule after 1821, the natives of the borderlands became citizens,
gaining an equal legal footing with European Americans. In practice, however, they were subject to the whims of local government, they were
compelled to pay special taxes, and their movements were sometimes
restricted. They were steadily forced off the land into towns and onto
ranches as laborers. In addition to typhus, smallpox, and measles, which
were prevalent in the colonial period, malaria and cholera took heavy tolls.
The exodus from traditional villages also caused fewer persons to be
considered Native Americans, as ethnic mixing and acculturation blended
identities and categories.

The impact of immigration and colonization from the U.S. Midwest,
Southeast, and eastern seaboard became clear by the 1830s. U.S. citizens
sought new wealth in the mining zones of Sonora and Chihuahua and in
livestock raising and commercial agriculture in Coahuila y Texas, New Mexico, and Alta California. The United States established wagon roads and
subsidized stagecoach lines. The U.S. government rapidly turned public
lands over to private holders throughout the West. Mexico actively encouraged U.S. migration to the frontier after 1821, hoping that an increased population would serve as a buffer between Mexico and the territorial interests
of the United States. Mexican policymakers generally considered the

immigration of national and foreign colonists to the sparsely populated North to be the best way to defend settled lands against the Apache and Comanche and to hold the North within the boundaries of Mexico's territory. They offered colonists land on much more generous terms than those of the U.S. government. Mexico allocated large, inexpensive tracts to settlers from other countries, including the United States, on the condition that they become Mexican citizens.

In Texas, Mexican colonization policy proved to be a mistake. The earlier U.S. purchase of Louisiana and continued expansionist sentiment and claims caused Spain to become concerned about the fact that, even prior to Mexican independence, colonists from the United States had begun moving into the region. Local Spanish military commandants, however, welcomed the newcomers as a defense against raiding indigenous groups. U.S. citizens, many of whom came with slaves, spread into the river valleys around Nacogdoches, Brazos, and Béjar. Following the Adams-Onís Treaty of 1819, which established a boundary between Spain and the United States, colonization by the United States became more purposeful. In the early 1820s, Moses Austin received permission from Spanish military authorities in Coahuila to settle colonists in Texas. His contract allowed him to bring three hundred families to settle on land near the Brazos River. Passage of Mexico's colonization law of 1824 and complementary legislation by the state of Coahuila y Texas in 1825 permitted Stephen Austin to take over his father's colony. The younger Austin brought twelve hundred families to homestead land along the Brazos River. Many more settlers from the East followed both legally and illegally. European colonists, African-American slaves and freemen, and eastern North American natives swelled the population of Texas. From 1821 to 1836 the number of Mexican settlers increased by about one-third, but that of other colonists grew much faster. By 1830, U.S. immigrants outnumbered Mexican settlers.

In contrast to the situation in Texas, U.S. citizens who migrated to New Mexico, Sonora, Sinaloa, and the Californias went initially as trappers and traders rather than as farmers and permanent settlers. The few who stayed frequently entered into commerce, mining, lumbering, crafts, and manufacturing; later they turned to farming and ranching. And the western borderlands, again unlike Texas, presented incoming U.S. citizens with an established civilian population of Spanish-speaking landholders, merchants, and craftsmen, as well as mission and Pueblo indigenous peoples who maintained the traditional practices of Mexico's colonial economy. Many newcomer merchants married into local families, thereby giving them access to local networks and economies.

During the brief borderlands interlude, there were three important changes in landholding patterns. First, there was a transition from the informal holding and use of land to formal, legal, written rights. Second, the period witnessed a shift from small family-run plots to large concentrations of land. Third, there was a virtual end to indigenous village possession of cropland, pasturage, and water, as title shifted to nonnative owners.

In Nuevo México, Governor Manuel Armijo granted large tracts of public land to private entrepreneurs in an effort to extend settlement to the upper Pecos, Canadian, and Arkansas rivers. Long-time residents of New Mexico towns and the Pueblo people contested these grants, defending the rights of communal ownership and protesting the sale of land to foreigners. In California, secularization of the missions released prime agricultural land and created a pool of cheap labor, both attractive resources for ambitious settlers. Between 1834 and 1846 the Mexican governors of California awarded seven hundred private land grants, over 90 percent of all grants issued during the combined Spanish and Mexican periods. Through marriage and business arrangements, U.S. entrepreneurs allied themselves with the local merchant and landholding elite and began to purchase land for investment and speculation.

In the Mexican North, too, the period saw the emergence of vast landholdings. In the northeastern states, extended families came to control huge estates. The combined property of the Sánchez Navarro family in Coahuila constituted the largest landed estate of the borderlands period. After independence, the Sánchez Navarros doubled their colonial inheritance, mainly through foreclosure on loans to other owners of large estates. In 1840 the family acquired the Marquisate of Aguayo, making it the greatest landowner of Mexico, with holdings of over fifteen million acres.

CONFLICT BETWEEN THE
UNITED STATES AND MEXICO

By the early 1830s the experience in Texas had convinced Mexican policymakers that allowing U.S. settlers to grow to a majority in its northern frontier posed a grave danger to the new nation. By this time, immigrants from the United States outnumbered all others in Texas and Alta California. In an attempt to control immigration and bring the northern frontier firmly into its sphere of influence, the Mexican government abolished slavery and imposed high taxes. And in a move that irritated the local settlers, the government began to use convicts to settle the region.

At the same time, the sentiment of Manifest Destiny was sweeping the United States. There was a widespread belief among U.S. citizens—from frontier people to New England poets, northern abolitionists, and southern slaveholders—that it would be beneficial to both countries to absorb Mexico into the United States. Expansion was a pervasive idea in the U.S. culture of the time, widely promoted in newspapers and political speeches. The United States repeatedly offered to buy Texas; Mexico steadily refused to sell territory clearly belonging to that nation under the 1819 Adams-Onís Treaty. Finally, Mexico sent an army to Texas in an attempt to bring the region back into the national fold. When Texas and Mexico went to war, the United States refused to intervene; despite its official neutrality, however, it looked with favor on the volunteers and weapons that poured into Texas to aid the independence movement. Even without overt U.S. support, Texas won its independence in April 1836. Britain, France, and the United States recognized Texas independence the following year.

For the next nine years, Texas defended its sovereignty against constant saber rattling in Mexico. For its part the United States placed the Texas issue on a back burner until the early 1840s, when increasing European interest in the new republic fueled U.S. concerns about European expansion into the region. California, with its access to the Pacific Ocean for whaling and trade, began to attract the attention of U.S. policymakers. U.S. interest in the West Coast sharpened when France and Great Britain expressed interest in the property. The United States offered to buy California for the price of outstanding U.S. claims against Mexico, but the Mexican government, still outraged over the loss of Texas, declined.

Diplomatic relations between Mexico and the United States deteriorated during the early 1840s. Mexico refused to discuss its debt with U.S. creditors or to reopen negotiations on the boundary established in the 1819 treaty. U.S. policymakers were alarmed by the perceived threat of the potential sale of California by Mexico to Great Britain. Tensions increased when the United States annexed Texas in 1845, an act that Mexico perceived as a declaration of war. Strong factions within Mexico that welcomed a war with the United States influenced other leaders to reject offers of peace; there was a great deal of confidence in the Mexican military's ability to resist the United States. Annexation of Texas became the final act severing the tenuous connection between the two countries. After a skirmish on land that clearly belonged to Mexico, armies from both sides hurriedly moved to the Texas-Mexico border, each preparing for the hostilities that broke out in April 1846.

Between 1846 and 1848 the U.S.-Mexican war was fought to a stalemate. Winfield Scott, commander of the U.S. forces in Mexico, occupied Mexico City and forced López de Santa Anna to terms of agreement. Both sides could make further gains only by bargaining. The occupation of its capital was a great humiliation to Mexico, but the war also cost many U.S. soldiers' lives. Although an All Mexico movement in the United States advocated taking the entire country, some observers worried about the expansion of slavery and the incorporation of a large, mixed-ethnicity population into the United States. The conflict was formally ended with the Treaty of Guadalupe Hidalgo (1848) and the forced sale of one-third of Mexico to the United States. In 1853 the Gadsden Purchase completed the parcelization of Mexican territory. All told, about one-half of Mexico, including Texas, was lost to the United States by midcentury. The Treaty of Guadalupe Hidalgo established a new international boundary that had immediate consequences for people residing in the now lost territories. As many as 300,000 people, many of them Mexican nationals, lived in the ceded territories and in Texas.

EARLY BORDER PHENOMENA

Changes followed immediately upon the establishment of the new border. Many towns located on or near the boundary were transformed by the new reality. Laredo was divided into two, with Nuevo Laredo established on the south bank of the Rio Grande. Tijuana, although it remained a modest village of little consequence until the midtwentieth century, emerged in 1848, as small ranchers and merchants capitalized on the new back door to California. After the boundary was drawn, many Mexicans migrated south into Mexico, where they founded settlements along the border. This movement was abetted by the insecurity of land tenure and continued rapid U.S. settlement on the U.S. side of the border and by the existence of family land held by returnees on the Mexican side.

One of the most significant stimuli to the growth of border towns was Mexico's campaign to repatriate its citizens to the south side of the border. The Mexican government was eager to populate its border states in an effort to avoid further U.S. incursions into its territory. Beginning in 1848, Mexico began repatriating southwestern families of Mexican descent by providing them with free land. Commissioners traveled to California, New Mexico, and Texas to recruit interested families. Established towns such as Guerrero, Mier, Camargo, Reynosa, and Matamoros grew in population as new towns such as Nuevo Laredo and Nogales were founded. Families repatriating from New Mexico founded several towns in Chihuahua, including Refugio, Guadalupe, La Mesilla, and Santo Tomás. At the turn of the century, perhaps one-quarter of the Mexican-origin population in the northern cities consisted of *repatriados* (repatriates).

New border settlements also sprang up on the U.S. side of the border, across the boundary from repatriate communities, to take advantage of trading and smuggling opportunities. In Texas, Brownsville, Rio Grande City, Eagle Pass, McAllen, El Paso, Del Rio, and other small communities emerged and thrived. In Arizona, Douglas and Nogales grew as commercial centers. U.S. military outposts constructed along the new border also served to encourage the establishment of towns on the Mexican side, as was the case with Fort Duncan and Piedras Negras.

The most difficult border-region conflicts of the period involved land. Most of the Mexican citizens occupying land grants in the ceded territories held titles that were valid under Mexican law but were considered vague and inadequate by U.S. legal traditions. Such circumstances as frequent changes in administration and the slow motion of the Mexican bureaucracy made it difficult for estate holders to obtain clear titles. Within months of the beginning of the gold rush in California, the call was raised to "liberate" property held by Mexicans. Texas proved particularly problematic, since one of the conditions of its 1845 admittance to the United States had been complete control over its own lands. As a result the U.S. Congress approved the Gwin Land Act in 1851. The Board of Land Commissioners was established to analyze the validity of Spanish and Mexican land grants. Grantees had two years to present evidence supporting their titles to occupied territories; if they were unable to document their grants, the land became part of the public domain.

In California the law touched off an orgy of speculation and squatter intrusions, as settlers moved to claim "unused" rancho lands. Mexican estate holders eventually lost the bulk of their property to lawyers, banks, and speculators. In New Mexico, where most of the lands were grants held in common by residents of former pueblos, Congress authorized the surveyor general's office to determine the extent of pueblo holdings. By 1863 only 25 grants had been confirmed; by 1880 only 150 of 1,000 claims had been acted upon by the federal government. Two-thirds of all claims were rejected; eventually, only 6 percent of claims were settled in favor of Mexican-era estate owners. In the meantime, as a result of the bribery of corrupt officials and the activities of speculators, thousands of acres of village and township lands passed to the federal government and were then purchased by individuals or corporations. In 1856 a ruling by the U.S. Supreme Court held that, because the Treaty of Guadalupe Hidalgo applied only to territories held prior to its signing, the treaty did not apply to Texas. In the following years, most Mexican-origin *tejanos* (Texans) lost some part of their property through "a combination of methods including litigation, chicanery, robbery, fraud, and threat."[4]

In most conflicts between Mexican and U.S. landholders over titles, U.S. courts ruled against petitioners of Mexican descent. The Mexican government protested, demanding compensation for damages. Responses to such complaints were ad hoc and limited in scope. The biggest winners in the land grab were U.S.-owned corporations and the federal government. Private estate owners who built up great fortunes would later invest their capital in border mining, commerce, and industry. The government would use its vast public landholdings to spur development in the West.

Midcentury witnessed the first major economic boom on the border. In January 1848, not two weeks before the signing of the Treaty of Guadalupe Hidalgo, gold was discovered in California. Large numbers of people began moving north and west to take part in the prosperity of the region. Between 1840 and 1860, 300,000 people migrated west on overland trails. The nonindigenous population of California increased from about 14,000 in 1848 to about 225,000 in 1852. This increase fueled rapid growth and development of western agriculture, trade, and industry. In the process many border towns flourished as well, as they became swept up in the boomtime economy. The rush reshaped large areas of the border, as migrants passed through them. Many never made it all the way to California, settling in the border region permanently. This early boom would be followed by one after another with similar patterns and rates of growth.

During the midnineteenth century, the border region was officially recognized by the Mexican government as a special area with distinct and unique needs. Free zones, where goods could be moved back and forth across the border without paying any duty, were established in Tamaulipas and Chihuahua in 1858. Shortly thereafter the border areas of Nuevo León became free zones as well. These sectors led to an economic expansion on the Mexican side, as trade and consumption of U.S. manufactures increased. Untaxed trade was eventually expanded to the entire border region in 1885. Although the existence of the free zone in these states brought significant benefits to *fronterizos* (border dwellers), it provoked opposition, particularly from merchants, in both Mexico and the United States. Many

Mexicans from the interior argued, with justification, that the free zone stimulated smuggling into the rest of Mexico, that it brought unfair competition for national manufactured goods, and that it prevented the government from collecting import taxes. U.S. border merchants complained of unfair competition and large-scale smuggling into the United States as well.

NOTES

1. Miguel Tinker Salas, *In the Shadow of the Eagles: Sonora and the Transformation of the Border during the Porfiriato* (Berkeley: University of California Press, 1997), p. 17.
2. This chapter draws heavily on four draft chapters for the historical volume of the UCLA Borderlands Atlas project: Miguel León-Portilla, Susan Schroeder, and Michael C. Meyer, "Early Spanish-Indian Contact in the Borderlands"; Paul Ganster, Bernardo García Martínez, and James Lockhart, "Northern New Spain"; David Hornbeck and Cynthia Radding, "The Northern Frontier during the Early Mexican Republic, 1821–1848"; and Richard Griswold del Castillo and Raúl Rodríguez González, "Conflict and Development: The United States-Mexico Borderlands, 1848–1900."
3. Ida Altman, "A Family and Region in the Northern Fringe Lands," in *Provinces of Early Mexico: Variants of Spanish American Evolution*, ed. Ida Altman and James Lockhart (Los Angeles: UCLA Latin American Center Publications, 1976), p. 260.
4. Richard White, *"It's Your Misfortune And None of My Own": A New History of the American West* (Norman: University of Oklahoma Press, 1991), p. 83.

CHAPTER TWO | # BOOMS AND BUSTS ON THE BORDER

ECONOMIC DEVELOPMENT, 1880s TO 1920s

DURING THE COURSE of the twentieth century a group of small, scattered outposts along the international boundary between the United States and Mexico, isolated from national and international economies and from one another, have merged into one of the most economically dynamic regions in the world. How did the economy of the U.S.-Mexican border region, so peripheral in 1900, evolve to its present-day dynamism and importance? What are the distinguishing characteristics of this momentous change? This chapter examines the early period of the century to shed light on the border economy's twentieth-century transformation.[1]

THE FIRST BORDER BOOM, 1880 TO 1910

The twentieth century dawned on the border region with great promise. During the last quarter of the nineteenth century its economy had taken off for the first time. With the ascension of Porfirio Díaz to the Mexican presidency in 1876 and his recognition by the

United States in 1877, sustained political stability existed along the international line for the first time since Mexico's independence in 1821. Díaz imposed law and order with an eye toward promoting economic development: "Order and Progress" became the motto of his thirty-four-year rule.

Responding to the novel political stability in Mexico, U.S. capital spurred the development of railroads, mining operations, export agriculture, and commercial endeavors throughout the border region. Porfirian Order and Progress led to an average annual growth rate of 8 percent per year between 1884 and 1900—the longest sustained period of economic growth in Mexico's history as an independent state. In the last quarter of the nineteenth century, closer ties between Mexico and the United States were accompanied by ever increasing exchange and interdependence in the border region.

The extractive economy of the border region, exemplified early on by colonial silver mining and the nineteenth-century gold rush, was transformed by three principal factors in the late nineteenth century. First, inexpensive transportation by rail revolutionized the relationship between border production and markets. Second, distant markets for border commodities had developed. Silver, copper, salt, lead, and other mineral products; lumber; commercial agricultural products such as wheat and cotton; and livestock were all in great demand as both the U.S. and Mexican economies grew. Border residents increasingly shipped most of what they produced to faraway buyers. Third, labor and capital for extractive activities, both of which originated outside the region and created a distinctly dependent border economy, increased in quantity and flexibility.

The most far-reaching transformation of the border region in the late nineteenth century resulted from the construction of a railroad network that connected the Mexican North and the U.S. Southwest with the major commercial and population centers in each country. Completion of the first transcontinental line by the Central and Union Pacific railroads in 1869 spurred the formation of many other rival lines throughout the West. The Atchison, Topeka, and Santa Fe and the Southern Pacific established major routes in the Southwest that linked most of the important population centers in the border region with one another and with eastern markets.

The first transcontinental railroad to pass directly through the border region was completed in 1881, linking the area to the western and eastern seaboards of the United States. Between 1876 and 1910 the amount of track laid in Mexico increased exponentially. Often the railroad tied Mexican communities more closely to the United States than to the Mexican interior; railroad lines in Sonora, for example, did not reach south to Guadalajara until 1909. By 1900 the Mexican North boasted more miles of track than any other region of Mexico—more than sixty-five hundred kilometers, which constituted one-half the national total.

The iron horse significantly boosted the economic importance of the regions through which it passed. El Paso, Texas, for example, suddenly became a key commercial hub for both the United States and Mexico. Prior to the arrival of the railroad, El Paso was a town of about 800 people. When news spread that the railroad was coming in 1880, a floating population of recent arrivals doubled the size of El Paso. "Bankers, merchants, capitalists, real estate dealers, cattlemen, miners, railroad men, gamblers, saloon keepers, and sporting people of both sexes flocked to town. They came in buggies, hacks, wagons, horseback, and even afoot. There was not half enough hotel accommodations to go around, so people just slept and ate any old place."[2] In the four decades following the arrival of the railroads, the population of El Paso grew to 80,000, transforming the town into a city with vibrant transportation, mining, trade, and livestock sectors.[3] The railroad profoundly affected land values in El Paso—lots jumped from 100 dollars an acre to 200 dollars per front foot—as both U.S. citizens and Mexicans moved to the area.[4] Between 1885 and 1910 the value of imports and exports passing through the city increased by a factor of seven.

In the interior of the border zone, too, the arrival of the railroad had a great impact on towns. Salinas, Coahuila, for example, grew from a small community of 778 in 1877 to nearly 15,000 by 1910. During the same period, Nuevo Laredo, Tamaulipas, experienced a similar, though not quite so dramatic, expansion from 1,200 to 9,000 inhabitants. Nogales, Sonora, increased its population from under 10 to over 3,600 by 1910 solely because of its rail connection to the South. The arrival of the railroad shifted economic power in local societies all along the border. In Sonora, merchants found it necessary to develop new relationships with suppliers on the U.S. West Coast rather than rely on their traditional European purveyors.[5]

The railroads also increased the value of the border region's natural resources by connecting them to distant processing plants, distribution centers, and markets. With the rail link, mines in Arizona, Sonora, and Chihuahua could ship their ores to smelters in El Paso with no difficulty. Timber stands in the mountains of northern New Mexico and Arizona became lumber for new homes in southern California and west Texas. The railroads opened up lands for the expansion of agriculture as well. By the turn of the century the Winter Garden area of south Texas, the Salt River Valley in central Arizona, and the Imperial Valley in southern California were emerging as important agricultural regions, capitalizing on both new irrigation technology and links to markets. With the decline of the open range, the railroad also became essential to the prosperity of the rancher, providing access to larger markets for sheep and cattle.

Of these border resources, mineral products remained the most important and held the greatest power to shape life throughout the region. A new mining code in 1884 replaced colonial laws reserving subsoil rights for the state, and U.S. investors led the way in developing Mexican mining ventures. Daniel Guggenheim obtained a concession to build three smelters in 1890 and received further grants in 1891 and 1892. Guggenheim eventually invested 12 million dollars in mining projects in northern Mexico. Overall, the number of concessions increased from 40 in 1884, to 2,384 in 1892, to 6,939 in 1896. During the final years of the Díaz administration, U.S. citizens owned 17 of 31 major mining companies operating in Mexico, controlling 81 percent of the industry's total capital (British investors held 14.5 percent). Guggenheim's ASARCO (American Smelting and Refining Company) was the largest privately owned enterprise in Mexico. Mexican nationals held a few companies, among the largest of which was the Torreón Metallurgical Company, owned by Evaristo Madero, the father of future revolutionary and president Francisco I. Madero.

By 1908 the border states of Sonora and Chihuahua had become the most important mining areas in Mexico, rapidly increasing their output of gold, silver, lead, and copper. From 1877 to 1908 the value of gold production in Mexico rose from 1.5 million pesos to over 40 million pesos, and the value of silver production rose from 25 million pesos to over 85 million pesos. Much of that output was concentrated in Sonora and Chihuahua.

Several other areas of the extractive border economy boomed. World demand for petroleum increased with the invention of the gasoline engine in the 1890s. Two petroleum investors—Edward L. Doheny of the Mexican Petroleum Company and Whitman Pearson of the Mexican Eagle Company (El Aguila)—came to control major portions of the border oil industry. Commercial agriculture and livestock raising in northern Mexico also expanded, again with a significant infusion of capital from the other side of the border. California newspaper magnates William Randolph Hearst and Harrison Gray Otis both held extensive rangeland in Chihuahua.

Manufacturing expanded rapidly in the Mexican border states during the late nineteenth century. As an industrial center the city of Monterrey, Nuevo León, became second in importance only to Mexico City during this period. As mining towns boomed, Monterrey satisfied the demand for such goods as nails, windowpanes, bricks, cement, explosives, metal products, clothing, cigarettes, beer, and processed foods. Small family-owned and -operated companies catering to local and regional markets expanded to become large capital-intensive, vertically integrated firms producing for the national market. The giant steel foundry Fundidora Monterrey, established in 1900, was the first integrated steel plant in Latin America. In contrast to the situation in mining and in petroleum production, the capital in northern manufacturing tended to be Mexican.

The border region boasted valuable natural resources, a network of rail lines, and inexpensive labor, but control of its economy was in the hands of bankers, investors, and corporations in New York, Chicago, Mexico City, and London. A small share of profits flowed back to the border. As San Francisco amassed wealth and power in the wake of the California gold rush, it joined financial powers in the U.S. East and Midwest and in Mexico City in directing the border economy. The border region in this early period was an economic colony, sending its natural resources to more developed areas.

By 1910 about 25 percent of the foreign investment in Mexico was concentrated in Coahuila, Sonora, Chihuahua, and Nuevo León. Only the

Federal District had a higher proportion (63 percent) of the foreign capital in the country. By the turn of the century, U.S. investments in Mexico had risen to over one-half billion dollars, far outstripping the amount of European involvement. More than a thousand U.S. companies were engaged in Mexican operations, with more than 20 percent of their activities concentrated in the border states of Coahuila, Chihuahua, and Sonora. These investments marked the beginning of significant U.S. economic influence in Mexico. The Mexican railroads—the catalyst to the nineteenth-century border boom—were themselves built largely by U.S. companies and were financed by U.S. banks. The rolling stock, railroad ties, and engineers tended to be of U.S. origin. By 1902, U.S. companies controlled 80 percent of Mexican railroad stock. After 1908, responding to increasingly strident nationalism, Díaz began to buy much of the stock in an effort to Mexicanize the railroad.

The state of Sonora provides a striking example of the extent to which U.S. investment dominated the Mexican border economy. At the turn of the century, U.S. investors owned several million acres of land in Sonora and in neighboring Sinaloa. Additionally, U.S. citizens controlled the largest mining enterprises in the state, and they were heavily involved in commercial and ranching activities. Powerful U.S.-owned companies, such as the Cananea Consolidated Copper Company and the Sonora Land and Cattle Company, played an enormous role in Sonora's economy, exercising considerable political influence as well. In Chihuahua the situation was much the same; foreigners obtained millions of acres of choice agricultural, timber, and ranching land, and they invested heavily in mining enterprises. These were not exclusively enclaves of U.S. interest and activity, however. In Minas Prietas-La Colorada, for example, U.S. investment served as a catalyst for regional development in which local Mexican elites built subsidiary industries that generated significant profits.[6]

THE BORDER ECONOMY
DURING THE MEXICAN REVOLUTION

From 1910—the end of the Díaz regime—to the onset of the Great Depression at the end of the 1920s, the economy of the border region continued to develop in what had become its traditional sectors: mining, raising livestock on the vast and arid plains, small-time agriculture, and some manufacturing and petroleum production. But the development paths of the two sides of the international boundary diverged markedly in this period. While the Revolution of 1910 held the economies of the Mexican border states in stasis—they neither grew nor contracted significantly as a whole—the economies of the U.S. border states boomed.

In the Mexican border states, the period from 1910 to 1917 was dominated by the convulsive political upheaval of the Revolution of 1910, which had long-lasting economic impacts for Mexico and for the border region. Peaceful political change was not firmly established until the 1920s, and the destabilizing challenges of regional strongmen remained until the organization of the first official party of the Revolution, the Partido Nacional Revolucionario, in 1929.

The violent phase of the Revolution did not destroy the Mexican economy of the border states, however. Despite the turbulence along the U.S.-Mexican border, trade and commerce continued. Though trade patterns and goods changed, the magnitude of commercial exchange increased significantly: the value of imports from the United States trebled between 1911 and 1920. The cost of exports to the United States was 57.5 million dollars in 1911 and 179.3 million dollars by 1920. What's more, official figures conceal the large amount of smuggling that took place. Manufacturing continued in many parts of Mexico throughout the decade, interrupted in some areas but not destroyed. The worst was over by 1915. Far more problematic was the negative effect on investor confidence; the conflict certainly did not encourage long-term investment in or optimism about the border region's economic future.

The petroleum sector boomed during the Revolution, with output increasing from 3.6 million barrels in 1910 to 157 million in 1920. British and U.S. investment in oil continued despite the violence. Most companies maintained production throughout the period; when oil fields came under the control of revolutionary groups, businesses paid taxes or bribes to stay in operation. By the end of the decade more U.S. investment than ever before was concentrated in the Mexican oil industry, having grown from 38 percent of total investment in 1911 to 61 percent in 1920. The Mexican petroleum industry, located principally in the border state of Tamaulipas and neighboring Veracruz, was producing over 25 percent of the world's oil by 1921.

The emergence of the oil industry in the early decades of the twentieth century also ranked as an important economic turning point in the U.S. Southwest. Oil had been discovered in the region prior to 1900, but little demand had existed until the invention of the automobile, improvements in heating and lighting techniques, and the use of petroleum byproducts in manufacturing. Texas quickly assumed leadership in the new industry, boasting major wells in the northern and eastern parts of the state by 1918. California also became an important oil-producing state after 1900, with extensive drilling taking place in the central and southern areas of the state.

Mining in Mexico did not fare as well as oil or manufacturing, however. Mines and equipment throughout the Mexican North were frequently located in areas of extreme turmoil, and, as targets of deliberate assaults by revolutionaries, some were destroyed. Transportation in this corridor was often interrupted; mining products were sometimes seized from trains. After reaching peaks in mineral output in 1911 and 1912, production levels decreased between 1914 and 1916. Declines were exacerbated by the outbreak of World War I and the disappearance of the German market, the loss of German cyanide (used to extract gold and silver), and a U.S. embargo on dynamite shipments to Mexico. It is estimated that mining production fell by as much as 50 percent during the revolutionary decade.

In the U.S. Southwest, in contrast, mining experienced significant growth. In an important shift, mining increasingly moved away from gold and silver to copper production. Copper was in steady demand for industrial applications; with the shift from precious metals to copper the U.S. West was evolving in step with the changing technological basis of national industrial development. In Arizona, copper production rose from 23 million pounds in 1883 to 719 million pounds in 1917. Mines and smelters at Bisbee, Morenci, and Douglas busily extracted and processed copper for use in the expanding electrical industry throughout the United States. Border cities such as El Paso became binational mining centers, processing and shipping ores from both sides of the border and selling supplies and services to mining companies and their workers. By the end of the 1920s the U.S. West was responsible for 90 percent of U.S. mineral production, excluding coal.

Mexican agriculture probably experienced the greatest disruption of all economic sectors. Crops were seized and distributed to revolutionary armies. There was a drastic decline in the production of corn and other staple goods. Famine accompanied warfare in some parts of the country-side. In the cities there was panic over staple food prices throughout 1915. Related was the lack of maintenance and the destruction of large portions of the transport infrastructure during the fighting. By end of 1920 the rail-roads—the great symbol of Porfirian economic progress—were in a state of disrepair. One-half of Mexico's locomotives were out of service.

In the U.S. border states, however, agriculture and transportation boomed during the second decade of the new century. New irrigation works triggered a dramatic rise in crop production. The Reclamation Act of 1902 prompted the U.S. government to construct large irrigation operations in the arid Southwest, causing desert areas to blossom. In the southern New Mexico-west Texas area, the Elephant Butte Dam project, completed in 1916, which included hundreds of miles of canals, brought 80,000 new acres of land under cultivation in the El Paso region alone. Steady delivery of Rio Grande water spurred an upsurge in cotton cultivation in El Paso, and the El Paso Valley emerged as one of the leading agricultural areas in the border region in the 1910s. All over the Southwest and West, farmers for-merly limited in their capacity to produce crops now expanded their agricultural operations. Large-scale water projects—Roosevelt Dam and the Arizona Canal in Arizona, the Imperial Dam for California's Imper-ial and Coachella valleys, and Elephant Butte Dam—established both the Bureau of Reclamation and the federal government as main pillars of eco-nomic growth in the border states. Western farming reached an all-time peak during the First World War.

At the same time, advances in food processing and the development of refrigerated railroad cars in the United States, which made it possible for growers to ship their vegetables and fruits to the vast eastern markets, created the potential for huge profits. In California, orange growers quadrupled their production between 1900 and 1920, and lemon growers quintupled theirs. The revolution in southwestern agriculture caused land values to skyrocket. The average value of an acre of California farmland increased from 25 dollars to 105 dollars during this twenty-year period.

The boom, brought on by water projects and demand sparked by World War I, was followed by a short-term bust in the early 1920s, as the agriculturally based economies of the U.S. West fell into a deep depression. The postwar depression contributed to a massive movement of people from rural to urban areas. Farmers who remained in agriculture shifted steadily toward more capital-intensive, mechanized farming practices in order to remain competitive in an era when farm commodities fetched low prices. Water projects and increasing mechanization led to the rapid growth of agriculture in California's Central Valley, which developed into one of the country's most important centers of cotton, fruit, and vegetable production in the 1920s.

The economies of U.S. border towns flourished during the second decade of the new century. A sizable portion of Mexicans who immigrated to the border region during the Revolution brought money and prosperity to the border towns they settled in while they waited for the Revolution to end. El Paso thrived as Chihuahua refugees brought their purchasing power to the border. Bank deposits surged, department store business boomed, and hotels filled to capacity. The city's assessed property value increased from 38 million dollars to 61 million dollars between 1914 and 1918. The El Paso Chamber of Commerce established a committee to help refugees cross the border and secure accommodations. El Paso also benefited from trade created by the Revolution. Arms attracted new customers from as far south as Zacatecas and Aguascalientes; local businessmen launched an aggressive campaign to attract Mexican buyers to the region.[7]

As many U.S. border cities thrived, some Mexican border towns declined. In Ciudad Juárez there was a continual flow north across the river to El Paso, as Juarenses (residents of Ciudad Juárez) left to find work. The disparity between the two sister cities grew more pronounced with the revolutionary fighting: ultimately, the "only available jobs around Juárez were in agriculture and making bricks for construction, both of which paid very little."[8] One observer wrote: "Juárez had featured many tourist attractions before the revolution, but the years of fighting had crippled it sorely. At every turn you come up in ruins—houses riddled with bullet holes or breached with shot and shell; a public library razed to the ground, a mere heap of stones; a post office badly damaged; and, opposite the Juárez monument, a brick building, roofless, with gaping windows and walls."[9]

Development in Mexican border towns tended to focus on entertainment and tourism. A reformist movement in the United States that gained strength early in the century drove significant sectors of the border entertainment industry south of the boundary during the revolutionary decade. Three cabaret operators forced out of Bakersfield opened bars in Tijuana and quickly became financial powers. Eventually, they financed racetracks, gambling halls, and a brewery in Tijuana and Mexicali. Ciudad Juárez also capitalized on this source of income. In the face of declining economic options and municipal bankruptcy, such opportunities were welcome.

In short, the Revolution retarded development in many economic sectors on the Mexican side of the border between 1910 and the early 1920s. Mexican leaders were preoccupied first with civil war and then with the politics of centralization and the reconstitution of the social fabric of a war-torn country. Mexican border states fell behind in several key areas in which the U.S. border states boomed. The disparity would continue through the twentieth century.

PROHIBITION ON THE BORDER

In the border region as a whole the 1920s saw the first stirrings of growth based on tourism across the international boundary. Prohibition in the United States, which came with the Volstead Act of 1919 (implemented after 1920), and restrictions on gambling and night life provided the impetus for the development of Mexican border-town economies based on the sale of liquor, on gambling, and on other services that could not be obtained legally or inexpensively in the United States.[10] Prohibition was the culmination of a moralistic movement that began in the United States in the nineteenth century. During the teens, large nightclubs, gambling casinos, dance halls, and the brewing, traffic, and sale of alcoholic beverages had been at their peak. The movement also represented a reaction against changes in U.S. society—such as women working, driving automobiles, smoking, and drinking—which were deemed undesirable by many influential guardians of public morality.

Prohibition affected the entire nation, but southwesterners, and in particular the residents of the cities close to the international boundary, had the option of crossing to Mexican border towns for pleasures not available in their own backyards. Seeing an opportunity to make money, many U.S. citizens and other foreigners obtained concessions from Mexican officials to open tourist-oriented businesses along the border. Prohibition encouraged owners of U.S. bars, casinos, and related enterprises to move their operations to Ciudad Juárez, Tijuana, and other Mexican border cities where few restrictions existed. For thirteen years, from 1920 to 1933, Mexican border cities boomed in an explosion of U.S. tourism.

The spillover effect was felt in U.S. border cities as well. In order to derive maximum benefits for El Paso, the local Chamber of Commerce advertised in national magazines and newspapers to promote visits to Ciudad Juárez. As a result, El Paso was frequently chosen as the site for national and international conventions. There was so much tourist traffic in Ciudad Juárez-El Paso that during a ten-year period two new international bridges were built. In addition, the El Paso Electric Company owned and operated an iron bridge across the Rio Grande, which produced a small fortune in tolls.

Just as Ciudad Juárez drew tourists from Texas and New Mexico, Tijuana enticed residents of southern California who sought such diversions as cockfights, bullfights, horse and dog races, nightclubs, casinos, bars, and prostitution. A prime attraction was the casino at Agua Caliente, established in 1928.

A large complex, it included gambling rooms, bars, restaurants, theaters for floor shows, a dog racetrack, a horse racetrack, a golf course, and an airport. Its owners, Baron Long, Wirt G. Bowman, and James N. Crofton, had operated night spots in southern California prior to Prohibition. The clientele comprised mostly U.S. citizens, especially prosperous Californians, among them many well-known movie stars of the period. Tijuanenses (residents of Tijuana) who worked at Agua Caliente as waiters, dealers, or bartenders during those years recall serving such stars as Clark Gable, Douglas Fairbanks, Jean Harlow, the Marx brothers, Jimmy Durante, Buster Keaton, Johnny Weissmuller, Bing Crosby, Dick Powell, and the celebrated gangster Al Capone. Many of the establishments in Tijuana were luxurious; their architecture reflected the romantic taste of the times, blending Mexican, Californian, and Moorish styles.

There was no shortage of tourist establishments on the Mexican border. Examples in Sonora included the International, Southern, and O.T.B. Bar-Restaurant at San Luis-Río Colorado; the Cactus Club and Americano at Sonoyta; the Royal Cafe and High Life at Nogales; the Foreign Club at Naco; and the International Club, Silver Dollar Bar, Curio's Cafe, and the Volstead Bar at Agua Prieta. In Chihuahua were the Central Bar and Fred's Place at Palomas; the Tivoli Gardens and Central Café at Ciudad Juárez; and the Riverside at Ojinaga. Coahuila included the Washington Bar and Newton's Cave at Ciudad Acuña and the Club International at Piedras Negras. And at Reynosa, Tamaulipas were the New York Bar and the Crystal Palace. The publicity directed at the U.S. public greatly contributed to the reputation of the Mexican border cities as Sodoms and Gomorrahs. An image largely created by profiteers, this was, in fact, the great attraction of the border towns. The problem with this effective reputation for sin was that a "black legend" of the border persisted for decades after Prohibition.[11]

Although Prohibition tarnished the reputation of the Mexican border, it also benefited the region. Revenues from gambling houses in Ciudad Juárez helped finance numerous city projects. The surge in tourism transformed Ciudad Juárez into the most prosperous city along the border, boasting a wide range of urban services, including electricity, sewage, and water services, pavements, and trolleys. Advances were made in transportation throughout the North. At Ojinaga, Chihuahua-Presidio, Texas, a new international bridge was inaugurated, uniting the Kansas City-Mexico City railroad line. Economic resurgence from tourism allowed the state of Chihuahua to develop some much needed public works.

Despite the economic and social progress promoted by Prohibition in the 1920s, Mexican border states suffered from uneven, superficial, and incomplete development. There were few systematic or lasting improvements in infrastructure, with the important exception of irrigation (in the late 1920s the central government devoted 6 percent of the federal budget to irrigation, most of it in the border area). Nor did the Prohibition boom underwrite investments in long-term economic enterprises in the industrial sector. Because of communication and transportation bottlenecks, border cities found themselves cut off from the rest of Mexico, nurturing instead commercial, economic, and social ties with cities on the U.S. side of the boundary.

In contrast, several broad and positive economic changes took place in the U.S. border states during the 1920s, including a spectacular growth in agriculture in the U.S. Southwest. Whereas nationally the number of workers in agriculture declined during this period, the border states recorded impressive gains in agricultural employment. At the same time, there was significant growth in nonagricultural activities and employment. Nonagricultural employment increased in the United States by 130 percent between 1900 and 1940, and the U.S. border states far surpassed that rate; Arizona recorded a 272 percent increase; California, 489 percent; New Mexico, 253 percent; and Texas, 392 percent. El Paso was one of many border cities that developed their industrial bases during the prosperous 1920s. Over two hundred factories in the city produced a wide variety of products by the end of the decade. Among the industrial establishments the most prominent were the ASARCO plant, which continued to grow in importance as a regional mining processing center, and the new Phelps Dodge refining plant, whose operations converted El Paso into a leading world producer of refined copper.

There were also considerable advances in the transportation sector on the U.S. side of the border during the Prohibition era. El Paso, Albuquerque, and Tucson were among the cities most affected by the increased integration of the Southwest with other parts of the United States by rail. These three cities evolved into important transportation and trading centers. Because of the mild weather and the unique Spanish-Mexican-Native American heritage, they also became tourist attractions. El Paso was in a particularly advantageous position to grow and develop. Enjoying railroad connections with central Mexico and with all parts of the United States, the city became a prominent transshipment and distribution center for raw materials and manufactured goods from Mexico and the U.S. Southwest during the 1920s. Many farming, ranching, mining, and manufacturing concerns in the surrounding territory depended on El Paso for a variety of supplies and services. Capitalizing on its border location, El Paso promoted trade with Mexico.

In Tucson the Southern Pacific Railroad and the Southwestern Railroad contributed substantially to the city's prominence in the Arizona-Sonora economy. Farming, mining, and ranching interests in the region looked to Tucson as a source of investment capital, processing plants, shipping facilities, supplies, and services. Again tourism figured prominently in the economy of the city, as local leaders publicized the plentiful sunshine of the Arizona desert. In the 1920s the Sunshine Climate Club promoted Tucson as the "Climate City of the Nation" and boasted that its tourist facilities were "the best in the West." With a membership of several hundred people and a hefty operating budget, the club conducted very successful advertising campaigns in leading national magazines. The "good life" available in the Tucson oasis appealed to U.S. citizens from other parts of the country, and soon thousands moved there permanently and many others chose Arizona as a vacation spot. Tucson also succeeded in luring large numbers of people who sought a desert climate for health reasons. Affluent patients were especially welcome, and every effort was made to make their lives pleasant and comfortable.

Tourism in the U.S. border states was different from Prohibition-led tourism in the Mexican border cities. People came to the U.S. border states to stay, frequently retiring on steady pension incomes. On the U.S. side the border boom towns combined tourism with deeper-level economic developments.

EARLY FREE TRADE

As early as the economic boom of the Díaz administration, border commerce was enhanced by legislation establishing free-trade zones along the Mexican side of the border. Recognizing the distance of border inhabitants from central Mexico, these zones allowed for the importation of goods from the United States at reduced or waived tariff rates. In 1885 the administration of President Díaz extended what had been a free-trade area along the Texas-Mexico boundary line to the entire border.

Always controversial, however, free trade experienced a series of government restrictions that reduced the benefits for border communities by the turn of the century. The Díaz regime justified its action, citing the increased integration of the border region with the rest of Mexico brought on by the arrival of the railroads throughout the North. The government eliminated the free zone altogether in 1905.

The end of the free zone changed life in many towns on the Mexican side of the border. In Ciudad Juárez, for example, once-prosperous merchants found the rules of the game changed. The city's turn to tourism through the construction of prominent tourist facilities followed the changes in the law. A bullring was built in the city in 1903, a racetrack in 1905. In subsequent years *fronterizos* lobbied for the return of free trade to the region. A 1911 article in a Ciudad Juárez newspaper pointed out that the poor state of farming in the Juárez Valley was due to high prices for oil—used to run irrigation pumps—imported from the United States. But Mexico City did not respond to such pleas until the 1930s, when dire economic conditions in the remote border states made duty-free importation of foreign products an absolute necessity.

It is important to note that the changes in the border region in the first two decades of the twentieth century, including the impressive advances on the U.S. side, were plagued by a major shortcoming: the region as a whole received limited returns from the raw materials it supplied to other areas. Ownership of petroleum fields, mines, smelters, ranches, and railroads remained heavily concentrated in the hands of outsiders. Industrial and financial decisions were the purview of investors, bankers, and federal governments whose interests sometimes opposed those of border dwellers. In effect the border region continued to function as an economic colony of the U.S. Northeast and Midwest, from whence the capital for sustaining the extractive and agricultural industries that dominated the region's economy originated. This situation was to change dramatically with the far-reaching impacts of the Great Depression and World War II.

NOTES

1. The first section of this chapter draws heavily on two draft chapters from the historical volume of the UCLA Borderlands Atlas project: Richard Griswold del Castillo and Raúl Rodríguez González, "Conflict and Development: The United States-Mexico Borderlands, 1848–1900," and Oscar J. Martínez and David Piñera, "The Mexico-United States Borderlands, 1900–1940."

2. James B. Gillett, quoted in Timmons, *El Paso,* p. 167.

3. Timmons, *El Paso,* p. 185.

4. Ibid., p. 167.

5. Tinker Salas, *In the Shadow of the Eagles,* pp. 5, 101.

6. Ibid., p. 177.

7. Martínez, *Border Boom Town,* p. 46.

8. Ibid., p. 50.

9. Quoted in ibid.

10. See ibid., passim.

11. Although Mexican authorities generally condoned vice-based tourism at the border, there were times when they acted to curb its negative impact. In 1925, for example, Emilio Portes Gil, governor of Tamaulipas (and later president, from 1928 to 1930), prohibited the sale of liquor on Native American *ejidos* (common lands) and in small towns to protect area youths. The construction of bars near churches, hospitals, schools, and workplaces was prohibited.

| # LIFE ON THE BORDER

SOCIAL CHANGE, 1880s TO 1930s

AT THE END of the nineteenth century the U.S.-Mexican border region was still sparsely inhabited; its population grew only slowly and fitfully. By the 1990s the ten states of the border region were among the largest and fastest growing in both Mexico and the United States. Moreover, the social importance of the border states increased markedly in the national life of both countries as the proportion of persons living in border states climbed to one out of every six. This chapter, which focuses on the period between the coming of the Mexican Revolution and the end of the Great Depression, addresses questions about social change: What were the main features of the social evolution of the U.S.-Mexican border region over the course of the twentieth century? What characteristics make border society unique and how has the social development of the border influenced national reality in both countries?

1880s TO 1910

In the late nineteenth century, rapidly expanding railroad networks connected the border region's natural resources to abundant labor supplies for the first time. The economic growth of the area was greatly facilitated by the availability of a large, inexpensive labor force consisting mostly of Mexican Americans, Mexicans, and Asians. In the mid-1880s the expansion of south Texas cotton acreage and sheep ranches relied on the annual importation by rail of thousands of Mexican migrant workers. At the turn of the century the development of open-pit copper mines in Clifton, Douglas, and Bisbee, Arizona, likewise rested on a mostly Mexican and Mexican-American labor force. In 1880s California the growth of agriculture in the San Joaquin Valley drew upon a multinational migrant labor force of Asians, European Americans, and Mexicans. The railroads that spanned the region were built primarily by Chinese and Mexican migrant workers.[1]

Large-scale Mexican immigration to the United States began in the 1880s, after the Mexican Central Railroad was connected with the Southern Pacific in El Paso. Enabled by the web of new rail connections, a mass migration in the late nineteenth century transformed the border's small village communities. In the U.S. West, the movement of millions of Europeans, European Americans, African Americans, Mexicans, and Chinese—for the most part by train—rearranged the social landscape.

The railroad brought an end to the border region's isolation from distant population centers. Towns like San Antonio and Los Angeles rapidly grew into major cities during the last decades of the nineteenth century; Los Angeles mushroomed from fewer than 6,000 people in 1870 to more than 100,000 by 1900, and San Antonio grew from 12,000 to 53,000 during the same period. As with earlier immigration to the border zone, the river of movement from East to West constituted the majority of the flow; smaller streams of migrants moved from central Mexico to the North and from the North across the border into the United States.

With the expansion of the railroad network, Mexico experienced a population boom on its peripheries, but especially in the states along the border with the United States. Mining, irrigated agriculture, and construction drew thousands of migrants to move northward by rail. The rate of population increase in the border states tripled, rising from 1 percent per year between 1857 and 1880 to 3 percent per year during the 1880s. The states of Coahuila and Tamaulipas doubled their populations between 1877 and 1910, while Baja California and Nuevo León quadrupled theirs. Pacesetters in urban growth in the north were the cities of Chihuahua, Hermosillo, La Paz, Saltillo, Ciudad Victoria, and Monterrey, with Monterrey's bustling industrial activities making it Mexico's fastest-growing city in the last quarter of the nineteenth century.[2] Only slightly less dramatic in their railroad-induced expansion were such cities as Sabinas, Piedras Negras, Muzquiz, and Linares. The improvement of port facilities helped spark the growth of La Paz, Mazatlán, and Guaymas on the Pacific Coast, and Tampico on the Gulf of Mexico. New and expanded mining industries in the north also provided a stimulus for population growth in such places as Mulegé, Cananea, and Navojoa.[3]

As a result of the new migration of the last quarter of the nineteenth century, the Mexicans and Mexican Americans of the southwestern United States—whether recent arrivals or descendants of settlers of former Spanish and Mexican communities—found themselves reduced to a minority and sometimes deprived of power and property by the many thousands of newcomers carried westward by the railroads. *Californios*—as native-Californian residents of predominately Spanish descent came to be called—declined from 82 percent of the population of California in 1850 to 19 percent in 1880. In Texas, *tejanos* remained a majority during the last half of the nineteenth century, but they became an increasingly impoverished majority. By the end of the century most had become unskilled rural laborers. Although frequently confined to unskilled jobs and segregated barrios, these residual social groups maintained vital and distinctive communities where their religion, language, and other customs stayed strong. They established newspapers, mutual aid societies, and sports teams that served their own social and cultural needs.

Native Americans, too, became increasingly marginalized during the late nineteenth century. Under Díaz the power of the Mexican North's indigenous populations to resist further incursions was definitively broken. The Yaqui people, who until the 1870s had lived in the agricultural valleys of the Yaqui River, were crushed by a series of ruthless federal campaigns that dispersed them throughout the state. In addition, thousands of Yaqui were deported to the Yucatán peninsula to work on henequen haciendas. The most feared Native American group both north and south of the border was the Apache nation, for whom nomadic raiding had become a way of life. Divided into many clans in southern Arizona, New Mexico, and southwestern Texas, the Apache had lived for hundreds of years in symbiosis with the Spanish-speaking settlers. From the 1860s to the 1880s, sporadic warfare erupted between border settlers and the Apache, the latter inspired by a series of charismatic leaders, including Geronimo, Cochise, and Mangas Coloradas. The U.S. Army failed in its attempt to keep the Apache on reservations. The standard cycle of broken treaties and massacres followed. In 1886, Geronimo surrendered to a joint Mexican and U.S. force in the Sierra Madre of Sonora. Apache raids continued periodically in Mexico into the 1920s, but after 1890 they came to an end in the U.S. Southwest.

A new border elite replaced older groups at the top of the social pyramid. The economic expansion of the North was accompanied by the emergence of many large and wealthy families. In Chihuahua, the Terrazas-Creel clan became one of the most important landowning families in Mexico. The family built its empire of wealth on land and cattle, as well as exports to the United States, and eventually owned ten million acres of land in Chihuahua, one-half million head of cattle, the largest meat-packing and flour mills in the region, the state's only brewery, textile and clothing mills, and an iron foundry. The Terrazas-Creel family dominated state politics for two generations.

CAUSES OF THE MEXICAN REVOLUTION

The Order and Progress brought to Mexico by Díaz between 1876 and 1910 (see Chapter 2) embodied the twin, mutually reinforcing causes of the Revolution of 1910 in the Mexican border states. The shape and course of violence in the North—and to some extent also in the U.S. border area—between 1910 and the 1920s ironically reflected signal accomplishments by Díaz. The intersection of long-term and short-term stresses caused the Revolution to occur when and where it did.

Porfirian "order" meant political centralization, which came at the expense of local privileges and customs. The force of centralization was particularly strong in the North, where the federal government had previously had only a tenuous grip on local activities. Throughout the North, an unusual degree of autonomy had been granted to settlers and frontier towns in return for holding the line against nomadic indigenous groups. With the withering of central authority after Mexico's independence, this autonomy had tended to increase.

Attacks on village political institutions under Díaz principally consisted in limiting this traditional autonomy. The central government began to appoint district and municipal officials instead of allowing them to be elected locally. Whereas villagers had historically chosen their own council members and mayors—the officials who allocated access to village lands, water, and pastures and who resolved conflicts in the community—Porfirian leaders took control of even minor municipal appointments. Porfirian politicians also introduced new taxation systems that replaced local with central authorities and old practices with new ones. In particular the northern states of Sonora, Chihuahua, Nuevo León, and Durango—all key foci of the Revolution—were brought under the control of Mexico City.

The dynamic of political centralization in Chihuahua is illustrative. There the Terrazas clan, working hand in hand with Mexico City politicians, destroyed even the pretense of representative local government over a period of a few years. From 1881 to 1911 a total of only eighty-six men sat in the state legislature, fifty-five of them on two or more occasions. In 1887 the state governor began to appoint *jefes políticos* (political leaders); two years later independent mayorships were abolished.[4] A 1904 law provided that the *jefe municipal* (municipal leader) be appointed by the governor. Because of this rapid political centralization under Díaz, social stresses in the North differed from the conflicts between communities and property owners over land tenure that characterized parts of central Mexico; in the North hostilities tended to express themselves as conflicts between common people and local notables over political power and prerogative. When conflict over power centered on resources, the fencing off of woods and prairies became the focus of the struggle.

Porfirian "progress" meant, above all, the rapid commercialization of agrarian and extractive activities. The key to this process was the expanding rail network that connected once isolated regions, such as the border states, to distant markets, vastly increasing the value of land in the region. Rapidly expanding circles of profitable agricultural and mining operations had swift and profound impacts on villages and towns throughout the North.

The case of Porfirian progress in Chihuahua reveals the sort of agrarian discontent that developed in the North in the period preceding the outbreak of the Revolution.[5] Colonial colonization efforts by the Spanish Crown had given settlers in the region 120,000 hectares of land, exemption from taxes, freedom from ethnic discrimination, and the right and obligation to carry arms. After independence these rights continued in autonomous communities. What emerged was quite unusual in Mexico: a territory of small landowners. In the late 1850s and early 1860s, hacendados, led by Luis Terrazas, began to buy up large estates. These landowners were not generally considered expropriators: they took little land from peasants, and they protected them against depredation by the Apaches and the expanding central government, refusing to send state resources to Mexico City.

In 1884, however, the first railroad connection from Chihuahua to the United States was established, and Terrazas, the patrician protector, was ousted. The rail link meant new markets for the state's mineral goods, cattle, and agricultural produce. As land prices increased, suddenly Chihuahua's village property became a very attractive commodity. The intense attack on the traditional rights of communities, followed by attacks on village holdings, eventually reduced the land of the original colony settlements from 120,000 to 20,000 hectares. These agrarian stresses, characteristic of both Durango and Chihuahua, would cause the two states to witness the largest popular mobilizations of the Revolution.

Under the Chihuahua governorship of Enrique Creel, Terrazas's son-in-law, a new law was enacted in 1905, declaring that all community-held land—not only collective grazing land but even houses—could be sold on the open market. The law required municipal governments to sell off all municipal properties, including housing plots, fields, and pasture. At the same time, a massive enclosure movement on larger haciendas emerged, reducing the lands available to inhabitants of the region for informal traditional uses. Terrazas had traditionally allowed people from neighboring villages on his property. Now these persons were forced to pay or see their cattle confiscated. Small ranchers lost access to irrigation water, increasing their vulnerability to dry spells. When revolution broke out in 1910, these communities were spearheading the movement in Chihuahua. Many men who assumed command were traditional leaders of the free villagers who had lost autonomy and access to land.

The long-term effects of Porfirian Order and Progress were accompanied by a growing discontent among working people throughout the North. Here again the railroad played an important role; after its extension through the border states, a well-consolidated mining, construction, and railroad labor pool flowed between northern Mexico and the U.S. Southwest. It is estimated that in 1908 between 60,000 and 100,000 Mexicans entered the United States to work in these sectors. In 1909 Mexican nationals made up 7 percent of the U.S. work force in mining and 13 percent in smelting. In Arizona the corresponding figures were 26 percent and 61 percent. By 1912, Mexicans were the main source of labor on railroads west of Kansas City.[6]

The ethnically diverse work force of the Mexican North and U.S. Southwest was often segmented according to geographical provenance, with the Mexican and Chinese populations generally assigned the least skilled, most arduous, and most dangerous work—usually at lower pay than other groups. Resentment festered around these points, exacerbated by rules that demanded respect toward foreigners and brought stiff penalties for their violation; *faltando respeto a un extranjero* (lacking respect for a foreigner) became a common pretext for arresting Mexican workers in the Sonoran mines. Industrial accidents were common, and labor conditions were generally austere. In 1909, to give one example, the Cananea Consolidated Copper Company reported 18 deaths and 769 accidents (47 of them deemed serious). There were no safety laws until 1912, and these were not enforced until the late 1920s. Everyday dangers to employees' health were frequently ignored. Sometimes workers also were caught in dependent relationships with employers; company store purchases were credited to employees' accounts or were automatically deducted from paychecks.

In general the commercial nexus in the isolated border states was characterized by strained social relations. Although general stores were not predominantly owned by U.S. or Chinese citizens, there was animosity both toward members of these groups who did own stores and against fixed prices. The small-time Chinese merchants, who, in contrast to their Mexican or U.S. counterparts, sold primarily on credit, were particularly resented.[7]

There was also a dramatic change in the late nineteenth century from traditional to more modern work routines in the Mexican North. The changing Mexican economy placed a premium on laborers who could adapt to consistent hours, routinized activities, and a new work ethic. At the same time, people were increasingly separated from access to subsistence farming as they became dependent on wage incomes. Many Mexican workers traveled regularly to the United States, where they were exposed to various labor-organization and agitation strategies, as well as to anarchist and socialist ideas.

Worker dissatisfaction in the North grew with the economic contraction of the first decade of the twentieth century. The Sonoran mining center of Cananea, for example, intricately linked to the U.S. economy, was negatively affected by the financial panic of 1902. Cananea workers, paid in pesos, found their wages worth half their previous value—U.S. staples were now at twice their previous cost. In June 1906 employees of Cananea struck, their grievances based in wage demands, particularly the elimination of the system in which Mexicans received less pay than did U.S. citizens. The manager of the company store fired on the protesting crowd, and, in the ensuing melee, workers killed managers and burned down the store. With the approval of the Díaz administration the company brought in by rail several hundred Arizona Rangers from across the border to suppress the strike.

The impact of Porfirian Order and Progress in the North was exacerbated by the sustained demographic increase in the border states during the same period. The population of Chihuahua doubled, an increase caused mostly by the number of immigrants brought by rail to mining towns. Reactions to these various stresses were diverse, including a series of uprisings in the 1890s, the most famous being that at Tomóchic.

Added to the popular discontents and disaffections that resulted from Order and Progress and helped incite the Revolution of 1910 was significant dissatisfaction with the Porfirian order by the elite in the North. The economic growth of the Porfiriato brought the Mexican North to national economic prominence but accorded it little commensurate political power. Few of the North's powerful families were as successful as the Terrazas-Creel clan of Chihuahua at gaining both economic and political power. The Porfirian political world was an exclusive one. By the first decade of the twentieth century, sectors of this elite were becoming increasingly disillusioned with Porfirian politics. Some began to push for reform. The classic example of the trend is Francisco Madero, the son of a wealthy Coahuilan land and mine owner, educated in France and California, who found that he could not break into local politics. In his *Presidential Succession of 1910* (1908), Madero gave voice to a widespread desire for greater democracy. He believed that a reform of the Porfirian system was needed to provide political opportunities for people such as him.

In addition to the long-term causes outlined above, important short-term causes of the Mexican Revolution existed in the border region. In 1907 a worldwide financial crisis sparked by a U.S. recession brought to a halt many of the economic gains of the Porfirian period. Few people in Mexico escaped the effects of this economic decline, which caused a crisis in mining and in the cotton fields of the Laguna region of the states of Coahuila and Durango. A shortage of capital led to many bank failures, and real wages fell dramatically. Social fallout in the Mexican North was particularly severe. The massive emigration of marginal and displaced persons that had occurred from central areas to the North in the period from 1877 to 1910 created a large pool of unemployed people in the region. Banditry became widespread and fueled the Revolution once the conflict had begun. Pancho Villa (discussed in the next section of this chapter) is the best example of the many men and women affected by these local blows.

Especially hard hit after 1907 were people and enterprises in the North that were intertwined with the U.S. market. The copper mines at Cananea, Sonora, the state's largest employer, began laying off workers in September and by the end of the year had completely closed down operations.[8]

As mines in the United States closed, Mexican miners returned home to face unemployment. Chihuahua, so dependent on foreign capital in its key mining sector, suffered a dramatic increase in unemployment. These changes served to accelerate the growth of militancy among northern workers, the general dislocation of the time proving more significant than ideology. The systems of credit and debt that had pervaded the lives of both rich and poor disintegrated. "After the 1907 crisis, the promise of development became increasingly illusory—as the mines closed, as merchants' sales plummeted, and as agriculture declined, old social cleavages acquired new importance."[9]

The world financial crisis of 1907—with its wide-ranging impacts in northern Mexico—was followed by a Mexican subsistence crisis in 1908–09. A serious drought in 1907 led to the loss of one-half of the wheat harvest in the Bajío (Mexico's breadbasket). Alarming reports of food shortages began to appear in the newspapers. Prices of staples skyrocketed, severely cutting into workers' earnings. Corn and wheat imports, which had been steadily increasing between 1902 and 1906, took off in 1908 and 1909. Because food generally constituted 60 percent to 70 percent of workers' household expenditures, food shortages and concomitant price hikes caused a dramatic decline in real wages.

The match that ignited the volatile mix in the North was a succession crisis at the national level. In an interview with foreign journalist James Creelman, Díaz—stating that Mexico was now ready for democracy—indicated that he would step down as president of Mexico in 1910. After months of political maneuvering, however, Díaz decided to run again. A group of middle-class political activists suggested Teodoro Dehesa, governor of Veracruz, as a vice presidential running mate for Díaz. Dehesa had an excellent reputation in middle and popular sectors, including those in the border states. His popularity reflected regional stresses: Díaz's proposed vice presidential running mate was Ramón Corral, a city boy associated with the interests of the capital and with the centralization and exclusion of the Díaz regime; Dehesa was believed to better represent provincial reformist interests. Shutting off every hope of the rising northern middle and upper classes, Díaz chose to stick with Corral. Thwarted backers of the Dehesa candidacy threw their support behind Madero as the only possibility for change.[10]

Personifying the growing disenchantment and resentment of a number of the elite factions, Madero called for a revolution against Díaz's exclusive political system after the elections of 1910. But to his considerable surprise, Madero was also able to rally to his side a wide range of popular groups either dissatisfied with long-term economic trends or negatively affected by short-term downturns of the Porfirian period. The mobilization of these groups drastically altered the nature of Madero's efforts to reform the political system, transforming the decade after 1910 into a period of civil war.

THE SOCIAL CHARACTER OF THE REVOLUTION IN THE MEXICAN NORTH

The best-known expression of Revolution in the Mexican North was the popular mobilization in support of Pancho Villa. Along with Emiliano Zapata, whose actions were restricted to south-central Mexico, Villa would come to symbolize the downtrodden Mexicans fighting between 1910 and 1917. Born Doroteo Arango, Villa came from humble origins, and much of his early history is obscure. Before the Revolution he appears to have made his living in a number of ways not uncommon in the North: through part-time and temporary employment of various sorts, cattle rustling, and perhaps some desultory banditry.

The motivations behind Villa's response to Madero's call to arms when the Revolution began were perhaps as much personal as they were ideological. But by early 1914, Villa commanded the dominant revolutionary force in the North, the División del Norte. Most successfully active in the states of Chihuahua and Durango, it made a number of early strong showings against federal forces. Middle-class revolutionaries were suspicious of Villa's proclaimed allegiance to Madero's cause. Venustiano Carranza, who emerged after 1915 as the leader of middle-sector groups desiring political reform, attempted to restrict Villa's actions by withholding coal and military supplies from his forces. Villa, unlike his contemporary Zapata, never presented a plan defining his objectives. This inability to publicize his goals, which left some historians questioning whether they existed, prevented Villa from gaining a national base of support. A mystery to many commentators and scholars, Villa came down through the twentieth century with an image as both a violent, villainous opportunist and a popular, populist hero of the common people of the North.

Villa's mobilization capitalized on well-established historical traits of border society. His army included a wide representation of border types, some of whom—such as the descendants of military colonists who had fought Apaches—had acquired particularly useful local skills and knowledge. The ranks of Villa's army were swelled by rural workers, sharecroppers, seasonal hacienda laborers, ranch hands—that is, exactly the sort of people affected by the long-term and short-term causes of the conflict. Many of Villa's followers may have regularly participated in marginally legal activities. As such they reflected the lawlessness and violence that, in the absence of centralized authority, were endemic in the border region. In Sonora in the period just before the Revolution, the number of people murdered in barroom fights frequently equaled the number who died in mining accidents.[11] Ideology of any kind seems to have been conspicuous in its absence among Villa and his followers. When in Sonora, for example, Villa's men did not distinguish between Mexicans and foreigners; they imposed their depredation on the entire populace.[12]

Villa's rhetoric and practice between 1913 and 1915 illustrate both his accomplishments and his contradictions. In December 1913, after his troops had dominated the state of Chihuahua and he had become governor of the state, Villa issued a decree to confiscate the land and other properties of the wealthiest and most-powerful Mexican landowners in Chihuahua, including the Terrazas. Revenues from land expropriation were to go to the public treasury to pay pensions to the widows and orphans of soldiers. Eventually, the lands would be distributed: one portion divided among veterans of the Revolution; another piece restored to earlier owners from whom the hacendados had stolen them; a third part to remain at the disposal of the state for pensions; and the last section to be used to provide credit to peasants. The main beneficiaries would be the descendants of the military colonists of Chihuahua. Once-autonomous municipalities would regain hacienda lands and receive new grants. All long-range plans were to be implemented after a total victory by Villa.

In actual practice under Villa the lion's share of confiscated haciendas was administered directly by and for the military high command, the best lands operated by Villa and his lieutenants. Some of Villa's men, such as Tomás Urbina, rented parcels to wealthy landowners; others rented land to sharecroppers on traditional terms. Even though Villa passed a law to prohibit the worst elements of sharecropping, his policy did not, on the whole, drastically alter the conditions of northern labor. For the most part the proceeds of the haciendas that remained under Villa's control were devoted to building his military machine.

Villa did devote some portion of hacienda income to social purposes but generally in a haphazard manner. When he took Chihuahua City, he gave each poor person in the city clothing, shoes, and other apparel taken from a large store confiscated from Spaniards, and from other stores he distributed candy to children. Once he became governor of Chihuahua, Villa decreed low meat prices (he owned a large meat-packing plant himself). He granted provisions to unemployed miners and other workers; he provided meat, milk, and bread to centers run by nuns for poor children. Wheat and maize from confiscated estates were sold at reduced prices. He made plans for further agrarian reforms, but he never carried them out (until mid-1914, Villa accepted the authority of Carranza, who did not yet desire a thoroughgoing agrarian reform).

Villa is famous in border history for a series of incidents that shattered the fragile peace between Mexico and the United States and brought the two countries to the brink of war. He became enraged at the United States for recognizing Carranza as official head of the revolutionary forces and for imposing an embargo on arms shipments for Carranza's rivals. The last straw came when the United States authorized Carranza to transport troops through the U.S. border states, enabling them to repel Villa at Agua Prieta, Sonora. By fall 1915, Villa's strength and status had declined drastically. On January 10, 1916, Villa's soldiers took sixteen U.S. engineers off a train in Santa Ysabel, Chihuahua, and killed them. On March 9, 1916, approximately five hundred Villistas attacked the isolated hamlet of

Columbus, New Mexico, killing and injuring U.S. civilians and soldiers alike. In response, General John J. Pershing led six thousand U.S. troops into Mexico in pursuit of Villa, angering Mexicans who found themselves face to face with armed foreigners. Two skirmishes at Parral and Carrizal, Chihuahua, produced casualties on both sides. The crisis escalated; a U.S. invasion of Mexico seemed imminent, but the two nations engaged in diplomatic negotiations. After prolonged and acrimonious talks, the conflict was resolved. In February 1917, having failed to capture or even catch sight of Villa, the U.S. troops withdrew.

Popular mobilization under Villa was accompanied by an elite mobilization in the Mexican border states. As a result of their activities during the Revolution, upper-class northerners came to dominate Mexico's political landscape for the first time. The main elite leaders of the Revolution and of the postrevolutionary rebuilding of the 1920s—Madero, Carranza, Obregón, Calles, Portes Gil, and Rodríguez—were from border states. The Northern Dynasty, as they came to be called, represented the new economic forces that emerged in the Mexican boundary region during the Porfiriato. Essential to the formation of these forces, the border experience would prove vital to the priorities and policies of the central government until the 1930s.

THE REVOLUTIONARY PERIOD
ON THE U.S. SIDE OF THE BORDER

The outbreak of violence in Mexico posed a number of important problems for the United States. As conflicts spawned by the Revolution escalated and spilled over the boundary, relations between the two nations deteriorated. Throughout the decade both revolutionary and counterrevolutionary elements made use of the U.S. border states to promote schemes for seizing power in Mexico. These activities prompted the government in Washington to impose arms embargoes and invoke neutrality laws. Meanwhile, U.S. citizens along the U.S.-Mexico border continued to suffer property loss and personal injury.

Revolutionary instability also affected local business and social life along the international boundary. Texas, where large numbers of people shared the border was particularly hard hit. As Revolution broke out in Mexico, peace along the Texas border began to unravel. The twin cities of Ciudad Juárez-El Paso and Matamoros-Brownsville became staging areas for incursions into Mexico. The arms trade flourished—the value of legal exports of firearms jumped from 270,832 dollars in 1911 to 1.3 million dollars in 1915.[13] Additional weapons were smuggled across the border. Battles between *federales* and *insurrectos* in 1911 heightened tensions along the Baja California-California, the Sonora-Arizona, and the Texas-Chihuahua borders. At the Texas-Tamaulipas frontier such traditional illegal activities as smuggling, gunrunning, and cattle rustling were overshadowed by organized banditry and raiding.

In at least one case, conditions in the U.S. border states, similar in many ways to conditions in Mexico, produced a popular mobilization. South Texas in particular was ripe for violence, if not revolution.[14] Since 1848 the Mexican-origin population in south Texas had experienced profound changes. Annexation had introduced a new elite of U.S. merchants, officials, and ranchers. At first the Mexican ranch society, which had developed over the course of nearly two centuries, was able to accommodate these developments; intermarriages pervaded all levels of society. By the early 1900s, however, this situation had begun to shift.

In the early twentieth century, rapid economic change came to south Texas. The arrival of the railroad and the exhaustion of homestead lands in the Midwest made the more arid regions of south Texas increasingly attractive to farmers. Irrigation works and dry farming techniques abetted development. The combined forces of the railroad, which expanded markets, and irrigation, which extended growing seasons and areas, transformed the region. Irrigated land increased from 54,673 acres in 1909 to 228,020 acres in 1919. In Texas as a whole this constituted a 32 percent jump, but the increase was 317 percent in the Lower Rio Grande Valley and 663 percent in Hidalgo County.

A large migration of midwestern and northern farmers to south Texas followed. This demographic shift, combined with the economic changes, led to the gradual eclipsing of the Mexican ranching population. The population of the Lower Rio Grande Valley nearly doubled between 1900 and

1920, with the greatest increase occurring after 1910. Hidalgo County experienced a demographic explosion—450 percent—during the same period. The proportion of U.S. citizens rose from 12 percent to 35 percent. Urban and rural property values soared.

These changes were met by a brief flash of armed insurrection in Texas between 1915 and 1917. The conflict was centered in the controversy surrounding the discovery of the Plan de San Diego. The plan, which called for an armed uprising against the U.S. government on February 20, 1915, apparently had its origins in the south Texas town of San Diego, a community with a majority (75 percent) Mexican-origin population. Supporters of the plan intended to reclaim the territory lost in 1848—Texas, New Mexico, Arizona, Colorado, and California. This region would first become an independent republic and would then be incorporated into Mexico. Every U.S. male over the age of sixteen would be put to death. Backers of the plan were restricted to Native Americans, Latinos, African Americans, and Japanese. Once the territory was liberated, six states bordering it would be turned over to the African Americans. The plan promised indigenous groups that, in return for their support, their ancestral territories would be restored to them.

U.S. authorities discovered the Plan de San Diego in early 1915, when Basilio Ramos, one of its authors, was arrested in McAllen, Texas, while trying to organize the uprising. Ramos jumped bail and fled across the border to Matamoros, but others pursued the plan's objectives by initiating raids against south Texas residents in the summer of 1915. Hundreds were killed, thousands were dislocated, and property worth millions of dollars was destroyed in a small area. It is difficult to determine, however, which attacks were perpetrated by adherents of the plan and which were the work of independent bands with separate motives. Groups ranging from twenty-five to one hundred men led incursions, including train derailments, bridge burnings, and the sabotage of irrigation pumping plants.

By the end of 1917 an uneasy calm had been achieved. Vigilantism in south Texas played a major role in the reduction of violence, and with the end of fighting in Mexico the south Texas movement lost its staging areas. The people of the region paid a heavy price. The raids, which had reinforced existing hatreds, led to severe repression of and general discrimination against Mexican Americans. Lynchings, hangings, shootings, and other forms of execution perpetrated by unscrupulous lawmen, soldiers, and vigilantes caused the loss of many innocent lives. The Texas Rangers exceeded their authority in many cases, submitting suspected lawbreakers, particularly those of Mexican descent, to unrestrained brutality.

The Plan de San Diego had international repercussions. Carranza apparently used the border troubles in Texas to his advantage in his attempts to gain U.S. recognition for his floundering government. When he finally received de facto recognition in October 1915, the organized raids associated with the plan stopped. Whether Carranza actually instigated or encouraged the 1915 violence is not certain, but following U.S. recognition of the Carranza regime, the border enjoyed a period of relative calm. The Plan de San Diego and the events in south Texas highlight the ease with which the border is transcended by social phenomena. Not only did ideas, arms, troops, and goods flow back and forth but similar conditions appear to have engendered similar social stresses and responses on both sides of the border as well.

TRANSBOUNDARY POPULATION MOVEMENTS DURING REVOLUTION, PROHIBITION, AND DEPRESSION

The Revolution of 1910 was one of the greatest early stimuli to population movement and growth along the border. In its violent phase, from 1910 to 1920, it constituted a major push for Mexican migrants caught in the shifting path of disruption and destruction. The U.S. economic boom resulting from preparation for World War I created a complementary migrant pull in both field and factory, drawing people from both the United States and Mexico to the U.S. border states. And the railroads that had linked Mexico to the United Sates in the 1880s provided inexpensive transportation northward. It is estimated that between 1900 and 1930 almost 10 percent of Mexico's population migrated north to the United States.

The number of persons crossing the border into the United States rose significantly after the outbreak of the Revolution. In 1912 alone 23,238 Mexicans entered the United States. Legal immigration to the United States from 1910 to 1920 amounted to 890,371, a figure that includes both legal immigrants and temporary workers (206,000 legal immigrants; 628,000 temporary workers). Many others came as refugees and as undocumented workers. The widespread poverty and hunger caused by the revolution triggered the displacement of countless people. Conditions were poor in the rural areas, where food shortages frequently followed revolutionary violence. In cities common people waited hours for the opportunity to purchase provisions, and urban food riots erupted in areas of the North.

A wide variety of people were pushed north during the Revolution. Most were unskilled workers; about one-half were either migrants without jobs, women, or children. But there were also professionals, teachers, architects, and lawyers. Middle- and upper-class persons who entered the United States in search of political asylum settled in such cities as San Antonio, El Paso, Tucson, and Los Angeles. Directly on the border it was not unusual for a whole town of people—poor and rich alike—to cross to the other side before, during, or after a military battle in the area. In October 1913, for example, eight thousand people went from Piedras Negras to Eagle Pass.

The impact of the Revolution on migrant flows was reflected in the modest growth recorded by four of the Mexican border states and the population loss recorded by the other two between 1910 and 1921. On the U.S. side, population increased much more rapidly during the Revolution in Mexico as a result of the considerable economic opportunities throughout the southwestern and western regions of the United States. The U.S. economic boom during World War I offered the unemployed jobs and good wages in the border region.

Until 1917 the only people who were not legally permitted to cross the border were beggars, the physically and mentally disabled, paupers, criminals, anarchists, those deemed incapable of earning a living, and prostitutes. In 1917 the United States passed an Immigration Act, which established several tests for migrants (among them a literacy test) as well as a head tax of eight dollars. As commercial farming expanded and growers' demands for labor increased, however, restrictions for Mexican workers were reduced. One cotton company executive, writing to President Woodrow Wilson, said, "Personally, I believe that the Mexican laborers are the solution to our common labor problem in this country. Many of their people are here, this was once part of their country, and they can and they will do the work. . . . I personally find them, especially those with families, to be appreciative of fair treatment and to be deserving of it."[15] Employers throughout the Southwest lobbied hard for exceptions to the 1917 act with respect to Mexicans. The literacy test and head tax were lifted as a result of this pressure, beginning a pattern of crisis and response in border labor recruitment and in subsequent migrant flows that is still common today.

Labor contractors—despite a ban on their activities in the Immigration Act of 1917—were very influential in supplying Mexican workers to the U.S. Southwest. Stationed near the border, they approached migrants as soon as they crossed. During the revolutionary period migrant labor continued to dominate agriculture and railroads. In 1909 almost one-fifth of unskilled trackmen in the U.S. West were Mexican; by 1928 they constituted 60 percent of these workers. Mexican migrants also traveled far from the border states, working, for example, in the steel and meatpacking industries of the Midwest. The 1920s saw even more Mexican immigration to the United States than had the previous decade. A brief postwar economic downturn in the early 1920s eliminated many employment opportunities, causing Mexican workers to return, or be sent, home. But the boom of the mid- to late-1920s soon brought migrants back.

The Great Depression slowed these population movements, as hard times fell on the economy of the U.S. West. Hundreds of thousands of Mexicans lost their jobs in the United States, and tens of thousands were sent back across the border to Mexico. Depressed economic conditions in the 1930s along with an increase in anti-Mexican sentiment motivated U.S. officials to impose severe restrictions on the entry of immigrants and to pressure Mexicans already in the United States to repatriate to Mexico. A drastic drop in the number of Mexican immigrants entering the United

States resulted. One-half million Mexicans were forcibly repatriated between 1929 and 1935. Foreigners received the blame for employment problems, as local government officials sought to remove Mexican families from relief rolls.[16]

A large percentage of repatriated Mexicans remained near the border, posing a challenge to state and local officials in Mexico from Tamaulipas to Baja California. Often transportation to the interior of Mexico was not readily available or was unaffordable, stranding returnees in such cities as Ciudad Juárez. Many repatriates who ran out of money were forced to depend on charity to meet basic needs. *Juntas de beneficencia* (charity boards) were organized in many border localities to deal with the problems of the *repatriados*.

The Mexican federal government attempted to aid *repatriados* by allowing them to import certain possessions without paying a duty, by providing free transportation to some destinations, and by opening up agricultural colonies for those inclined to take up farming. Although well intentioned, the assistance rendered by the government in Mexico City often fell far short of actual needs. The government's promises surpassed its ability to minister to the large number of migrants. For this reason many *repatriados* remained close to the border, awaiting the opportunity to reenter the United States when economic conditions improved.

Many neighborhoods in border urban centers trace their origin to the arrival of repatriated Mexicans during the depression. One example is Colonia Libertad in Tijuana, which was settled beginning in 1930. Many of the refugees who founded Colonia Libertad settled unlawfully on vacant land that belonged to a racetrack complex in the process of relocation. The invaders resisted all efforts to remove them. The name Colonia Libertad attracted former Villistas and adherents of anarchist ideology. Its settlement pattern followed the U.S. model of large lots, wide and straight streets, and alleys for services. *Repatriados* who preferred a rural life-style settled in the Mexicali Valley, taking advantage of the area's growing focus on agriculture, stimulated by federal water projects and land programs.

The large Mexican immigration into the United States between 1910 and 1930 coincided with a resurgence in anti-Mexican sentiment in the

United States that only worsened during the depression. Attacks on U.S. citizens in Mexico and recurring border incidents during the years of the Mexican Revolution had influenced some U.S. citizens to call for major military intervention in Mexico. Many frustrated U.S. citizens took out their resentment on Mexicans and Mexican Americans along the border. Even when the violence in Mexico subsided and the potential for large-scale confrontation between U.S. citizens and Mexican nationals dissipated, negative attitudes toward Mexicans found expression in the debate over immigration that swept the United States during the 1920s. In the 1920s and 1930s there was growing opposition to unrestricted immigration into the United States, and, because of their expanding visibility in the labor markets of the Southwest, Mexicans became a principal target.

Despite the concerted efforts by labor unions and restrictionists who were motivated by concerns over ethnicity, the U.S. Congress excluded Mexicans and other Latin Americans from the strict quotas imposed in the landmark immigration acts of 1921 and 1924. The border states won the period's debates over immigration. The great need for inexpensive labor in the U.S. border region and the desire to improve relations between the United States and Latin America compelled the United States to allow Mexicans to continue entering the country with relative ease.

Pleasing to many U.S. border-state employers, the permissive policy caused distress in other sectors. Opponents of Mexican immigration cited economic, cultural, social, and ethnic differences to make their case. Organized labor, for example, complained that Mexican immigrants depressed wages and interfered with efforts to unionize workers. Other observers focused on an alleged inability and unwillingness by the Mexican people to assimilate into the mainstream culture. These themes, replayed ever since, still shaped debate on a constellation of policy issues at the end of the twentieth century.

In the first forty years of the twentieth century the population of the border region almost tripled, from a total of about 6 million in 1900 to nearly 17 million by 1940, an annual rate of 2.5 percent (see Table 3-1).[17] In 1900, Baja California, Chihuahua, Coahuila, Nuevo León, Sonora, and Tamaulipas had a combined population of about 1.4 million; by 1940 that

TABLE 3-1
BORDER-STATE POPULATION, 1900–1940

State	1900	1910	1920[a]	1930	1940
Baja California	7,583	9,760	23,537	48,327	78,907
Chihuahua	327,784	405,707	401,622	491,792	623,944
Coahuila	296,938	362,092	393,480	436,425	550,717
Nuevo León	327,937	365,150	336,412	417,491	541,147
Sonora	221,682	265,383	275,127	316,271	364,176
Tamaulipas	218,948	249,641	286,904	344,039	458,832
Mexican border	1,400,872	1,657,733	1,717,082	2,054,345	2,617,723
Mexican total	13,607,272	15,160,369	14,334,780	16,552,722	19,653,552
Arizona	122,931	204,354	334,162	435,573	499,261
California	1,485,053	2,377,549	3,426,861	5,677,251	6,907,387
New Mexico	195,310	327,301	360,350	423,317	531,818
Texas	3,048,710	3,876,542	4,663,228	5,824,715	6,414,824
U.S. border	4,852,004	6,785,746	8,784,601	12,360,856	14,353,290
U.S. total	76,212,168	92,228,496	106,021,537	123,202,624	132,164,569

Source: Lorey, *United States-Mexico Border Statistics since 1900*, Table 100.
[a] Data for Mexico are for 1921.

number had increased to approximately 2.6 million. The combined population of the U.S. border states grew from almost 4.9 million in 1900 to almost 14.4 million by 1940. For most of the period, Texas was the giant among the border states, but by 1940, with a population of nearly 7 million, California had assumed the lead. Most of the border growth took place on the U.S. side; the 1.6 percent per year increase on the Mexican side was significantly lower than the overall rate.

After 1900 the border region became increasingly urbanized, but the growth of individual cities varied considerably. The Mexican Revolution and the Great Depression significantly affected cities south of the Rio Grande, slowing growth or causing population declines. That trend also characterized the U.S. border cities, where both El Paso, Texas, and Calexico, California, lost population in the 1930s. Albuquerque, like El Paso and Tucson, lured many health seekers by advertising its dry and mild climate and emerged as the dominant city of New Mexico. Specialists in such diseases as tuberculosis and asthma moved to the border states to meet the growing demand for their services; modern medical establishments replaced the health spas and wintering hotels of an earlier era. Although the largest metropolises of the region developed at some distance from the international boundary, their growth owed much to their proximity to the border. Los Angeles reigned as the largest U.S. border city throughout the first four decades of the century, followed by Houston, San Antonio, and San Diego. On the Mexican side, Monterrey remained the largest border city, but, with a population of only 186,092 in 1940, it was far smaller than the leading U.S. cities. On the West Coast, Tijuana grew from a hamlet of 242 people in 1900 to a town of nearly 17,000 people by 1940. With a combined population of 146,000 in 1940, Ciudad Juárez-El Paso occupied the top spot among twin-city complexes at the border from the turn of the century onward.

NOTES

1. This section draws heavily on Griswold del Castillo and Rodríguez González, "Conflict and Development."
2. David Lorey, "Monterrey, Mexico, during the Porfiriato and Revolution: Population and Migration Trends in Regional Evolution," *Statistical Abstract of Latin America* 28 (1990): 1183–1204.
3. Griswold del Castillo and Rodríguez González, "Conflict and Development."
4. Ramón Ruíz, *The Great Rebellion: Mexico, 1905–1924* (New York: Norton, 1980), pp. 36–37.
5. This discussion of Chihuahua and the discussion of Francisco (Pancho) Villa in the next section of this chapter are adapted from Friedrich Katz's work, particularly his speech "Was There an Agrarian Problem in the Mexican North on the Eve of the Mexican Revolution?" (given at the Center for U.S.-Mexican Studies, University of California, San Diego, 1995); his "Agrarian Changes in Northern Mexico in the Period of *Villista* Rule," in *Contemporary Mexico*, ed. James Wilkie (UCLA Latin American Center Publications, 1976), pp. 259–73; and his *Pancho Villa* (Stanford: Stanford University Press, 1998). See also Alan Knight, *The Mexican Revolution*, 2 vols. (Lincoln: University of Nebraska Press, 1986).
6. French, *A Peaceful and Working People*, p. 43.
7. Tinker Salas, *In the Shadow of the Eagles*, pp. 187–88, 196.
8. Ibid., p. 239.
9. Ibid., p. 8.
10. Karl B. Koth, "Crisis Politician and Political Counterweight: Teodoro A. Dehesa in Mexican Federal Politics, 1900–1910," *Mexican Studies/Estudios Mexicanos* 11:2 (Summer 1995): 243–71.
11. Tinker Salas, *In the Shadow of the Eagles*, p. 193.
12. Ibid., p. 199.

13. Coerver and Hall, *Revolution on the Border,* p. 157.
14. The discussion of the south Texas rebellion is adapted from Sandos, *Rebellion in the Borderlands*; and Montejano, *Anglos and Mexicans in the Making of Texas.*
15. Coerver and Hall, *Revolution on the Border,* p. 134.
16. On repatriation see Balderrama and Rodríguez, *Decade of Betrayal;* Abraham Hoffman, *Unwanted Mexican Americans in the Great Depression* (Tucson: University of Arizona Press, 1974); and Guerin-Gonzales, *Mexican Workers and American Dreams.*
17. Implicit compound rate.

CHAPTER FOUR | # BOOMS AND BUSTS
ON THE BORDER

1930s AND 1940s

THE GREAT DEPRESSION and World War II brought momentous, lasting change to the U.S.-Mexican border region, transforming it, in the span of twenty years, from an economic backwater into a global powerhouse. The New Deal, designed by Franklin Delano Roosevelt to promote economic recovery and social reform, forever altered the economy of the United States, especially the West. Meanwhile, reforms of the 1930s touched off an impressive economic consolidation in Mexico, one that had far-reaching implications for the development of the Mexican border states. World War II brought dramatic economic changes to both Mexico and the United States, with significant ramifications in the border states. In both countries an active federal government increasingly provided the area with a stable foundation for rapid development and a way to free itself from regional dependencies—from the domination of the East in the United States and from the domination of Mexico City in Mexico.

THE GREAT DEPRESSION

The depression was a mixed blessing for the border region. Although it caused extensive short-term dislocation for people in both Mexican and U.S. border states, federal responses in both countries provided long-term investments in infrastructure and a precedent of federal support for regional economic growth. Depression-era infrastructure would prove to be one of the foundations for the area's wartime and postwar economic expansion. As in the case of the short-lived boom brought on by Prohibition, however, most depression-era benefits were experienced north of the international boundary.

During the early 1930s the U.S. border states, paralleling occurrences in other parts of the United States, experienced deep economic disruption as a result of the Great Depression. Banks defaulted, factories closed, businesses failed, and masses of workers lost their jobs. Throughout the Southwest, people from rural and urban areas struggled to make a living in an environment that provided limited opportunities. In El Paso, the Great Depression was first felt in the latter part of 1931, when a prominent bank collapsed. In the years that followed, many factories and stores went out of business, throwing thousands out of work. Between 1929 and 1939 the number of workers employed by major manufacturing establishments in El Paso decreased by 63 percent. The economic pressures became so great that many people left El Paso; the city's population fell from 102,000 in 1930 to 97,000 in 1940. Many Mexicans repatriated to their homeland when they could no longer make a living in the United States. Although Tucson suffered less than El Paso, the city still had to cope with major disruptions in trade, mining, ranching, and agriculture; tourism sharply declined as well.

Tijuana was also hard hit by the depression. One hundred and fifty of the town's commercial establishments ceased operation in the first months of the crisis. The majority of foreign owners left; some even torched their businesses to collect insurance (two dozen fires were reported in 1935). The number of border crossings declined considerably between the late 1920s and the mid-1930s, falling from twenty-seven million in 1928 to twenty-one million in 1934. In Ciudad Juárez, tourist expenditure dropped from 3.5 million dollars to 2.3 million dollars.

In the United States the most important and longest-lasting impact of the 1930s was the use of federal funds to underwrite infrastructure projects, which supported western economic development in both direct and indirect ways. The Great Depression brought hardship to the U.S. West, but it also brought Roosevelt's New Deal. The federal government subsidized both producers and consumers. Large-scale water projects, such as Boulder Dam, Hoover Dam, and the All-American Canal, provided irrigation, inexpensive electric power, and much-needed employment.

Both border states and border communities benefited from New Deal relief programs during the difficult years. The Civilian Works Administration provided employment for thousands of El Pasoans by implementing projects ranging from constructing roads to channeling the Rio Grande. The federal government also helped preserve the troubled Middle Rio Grande Conservancy District, an agency that held great importance for Albuquerque. With the availability of federal resources the District was able to undertake numerous activities that improved the environment for commercial agriculture in the Rio Grande Valley. With the arrival of New Deal programs, the situation in Tucson also looked up, and by the late 1930s the so-called Sunshine Capital of the United States was once again booming as a winter haven for people from the frigid North. New Deal agencies such as the Reconstruction Finance Corporation, the Federal Relief Emergency Administration, the Works Progress Administration, and the Civilian Conservation Corps invested heavily in a wide variety of endeavors in the western states, stimulating new or restarting disrupted activity in such important regional industries as agriculture, ranching, construction, and mining. Most significantly, large-scale water projects financed by the federal government during the depression led to the conversion of semiarid areas of the West into some of the most productive farmland in the country.

In comparison with other parts of the United States, the West benefited from a disproportionate share of the New Deal expenditures, with the border states receiving substantial grants and loans. Arizona and New Mexico in particular—which placed in the top five states nationwide in terms of per capita federal funding—felt the helping hand of the government in Washington. These events were the first steps toward a massive shift of federal resources to the western United States.

The world economic crisis of the 1930s prompted Mexican policy-makers to institute fundamental changes in the nation's economy. The federal government encouraged internal commerce by establishing associations of merchants and promoting greater integration of the country through improved transportation networks. Banks were reorganized and credit was extended to sectors in need of it, especially agriculture. Import-substitution measures protected existing industries and stimulated new manufacturing activities.

During the Lázaro Cárdenas administration (1934–1940) in particular, Mexico experienced profound economic transformations, which had striking consequences for the northern border states. In the North, land reform, one of the principal objectives of the Cárdenas government, led to the expropriation of millions of hectares and the creation of many communally owned and farmed *ejidos*. By 1935 more than 181,000 *ejidatarios* worked in communal agriculture throughout northern Mexico. The years 1936 and 1937 were especially significant on the border, as large-scale land redistribution reached Coahuila, Sonora, and Baja California. In 1937, Cárdenas distributed almost 25,000 hectares of land to peasant families in the Mayo Valley and a total of 34,000 hectares to settlers and Native American villages on both banks of the Yaqui River Valley (later grants to the Yaqui, between 1937 and 1939, would bring the total to 450,000 hectares).

The government carried out one of its most ambitious agricultural projects in the Laguna district in the states of Coahuila and Durango. In 1937, land for 30,000 families was distributed, allowing for *ejido* cultivation of cotton, wheat, alfalfa, and corn. The government gave a major boost to agriculture by building dams to supply irrigation water to the *ejidos*. The construction of schools, hospitals, and community centers allowed for the provision of a variety of social services.

Land reform transformed the Mexicali Valley and the San Luis-Río Colorado areas, where for years the powerful Colorado River Land Company had claimed ownership of more than one-half million hectares. Unaffected by previous agrarian reform efforts by Villa or by Presidents

Carranza, Obregón, and Calles, the company had enjoyed effective economic and political control of the region from 1902 through the Revolution. By the mid-1930s growing Mexican nationalism prompted the firm to sell *ejido* lots to Mexican farmers. At the end of 1937 over 47,000 hectares had changed hands, benefiting 4,500 Mexican families who settled permanently in the Mexicali Valley. A decade later the government bought the remainder of the company's holdings, concluding the most important border campaign to provide peasants with land in the form of communal agricultural colonies.

Reclamation projects begun in the late 1920s and stepped up by the Cárdenas government during the depression created new and expanded old agricultural lands in northern Mexico. Between 1926 and 1940, irrigation projects created about 370,000 acres of irrigated land throughout the nation, with high concentration in the arid North.

In an attempt to stimulate tourism in the Mexican border states, the central government tried to rein in border vice. Especially after Prohibition was repealed in 1933 and particularly during the administration of Cárdenas, local and federal officials banned disreputable diversions. The *El Paso Herald Post* reported a transformation by the mid-1930s:

> Gone are the hundred-odd saloons, the downtown honky-tonks and brothels, and the open gambling. In the Tívoli Casino the visitor can no longer hear the click of dice, the riffle of cards, and the sing-song croupiers at the roulette tables. The place is closed by presidential decree. The Moulin Rouge, once the home of nude dances, is closed. Part of the building is being remodeled for a grocery store. Calle Diablo [a red-light district] is no longer a Mecca for El Paso night-life addicts. A few cabarets remain open on Calle Diablo, but most of the girls have moved to restricted zones. Juárez no longer has vice resorts on her downtown streets.[1]

A federal policy that held great importance for the North during the depression was the reestablishment of free-trade zones along the border. Cities like Tijuana and Ensenada, which strongly depended on U.S. tourism, were left economically depressed by the end of Prohibition in the United States. By the mid-1930s many casinos, bars, and related establishments had closed their doors. Because of their geographic isolation from the rest of Mexico, it was crucial that border residents be allowed to import U.S. goods without having to pay tariffs. Border-state policymakers persuaded the central government that without a free-trade zone there would be a significant decline in both population and local commerce.

As early as 1933 the federal government responded to the concerns of *fronterizos* by declaring Ensenada and Tijuana *perímetros libres* (free perimeters), where U.S. products could be imported without payment of the normal tariffs. Four years later the entire Baja California territory was designated a free zone, allowing the increasingly important town of Mexicali to benefit from free trade as well. In 1939, Agua Prieta and Nogales, Sonora, were included in the free zone, as was Baja California Sur. In effect the entire northwest border region had become a free-trade zone by 1939, stimulating commerce in every affected community.

WORLD WAR II

The Second World War ushered in an era of unparalleled growth in the border region. U.S. border states were catapulted forward by an outpouring of federal expenditure for defense, with the lion's share going to the states along the Pacific Coast and in the Southwest. The depression rapidly faded, as the nation's private sector expanded to meet both pent-up consumer demands and the needs of the defense machine. Federal spending in Mexico, though lower and slower than that in the U.S., nonetheless helped transform that country's North into an area of large industries and growing cities in the 1940s and 1950s.

During the three decades following 1939 the U.S. gross national product (GNP) grew at an average annual rate of 4.2 percent. The war effort was primarily responsible for this surge, and the federal government significantly increased its participation in the economy in order to bring the country to peak military strength. Federal expenditures stood below 10 percent of the GNP prior to 1941 but jumped to over 40 percent during the war. A significant measure of federal wartime spending was directed toward new commercial enterprises on the cutting edge of technology. Government investments in aircraft, electronics, and nuclear weapons bolstered not only the nation's war effort but also the extraordinary growth of the allied nuclear power, rocketry, communications, computer, and chemical industries. Technology-based firms such as Boeing, Lockheed, Douglas, and Westinghouse owe their industrial leadership to federal outlays during World War II. The war, therefore, more so than even the Great Depression, made the federal budget an engine of growth and change. Although this process affected the entire country, it especially influenced the border states.

Prior to 1940 the U.S. border economy depended heavily on agriculture and mining and relatively little on manufacturing. The western United States as a whole contributed approximately 11 percent of the U.S. manufacturing value added. The four border states contributed even less, and New Mexico ranked last in the nation. This primary-sector emphasis of the prewar border economy had always made development in the region particularly dependent on the government in Washington, and the expenditures following the outbreak of the war served to reinforce this relationship.

The border economy's primary-sector emphasis was transformed with the impact of federal wartime spending. The government invested some 40 billion dollars in the western United States during the war, including 29 billion dollars for weapons and 7 billion dollars for supply depots, training camps, and a variety of other military facilities. A single border state, California, received 10 percent of all federal monies expended during the war. From 1940 to 1946, 360 billion federal dollars were spent within the continental United States, 35 billion dollars in California alone. In 1930 the government in Washington had spent just 191 million dollars in California; by 1945 federal expenditure in California had mushroomed to 8.5 billion dollars.

Federal monies launched southern California as the center of the nation's war aircraft industry, and the San Francisco Bay area emerged as a focus of wartime shipbuilding efforts. By the conflict's end, ships and airplanes had become California's second most important products, behind only food production in terms of value added and people employed. And, since ships and aircraft required steel, Roosevelt strengthened the regional economy by supporting the establishment of Kaiser steel factories in the Los Angeles suburb of Fontana.

During World War II, the federal government funded new research clusters such as the Lawrence Radiation Laboratory at Berkeley and the Los Alamos Scientific Laboratory in New Mexico. Major research universities such as Stanford, the California Institute of Technology, and the University of California at Berkeley and at Los Angeles received lavish federal grants during the war. These institutions also attracted a number of firms that settled nearby and invested their energies in aerospace, advanced electronics, rocketry, and similar ventures.

Wartime expenditures accelerated the region's shift from an economy based primarily on extractive industries to a diversified economy strongest in manufacturing and service industries. Just as was the case with the more traditional agricultural and mining activities, the new manufacturing sector depended heavily on the federal budget; its lead businesses tended to be high-tech firms associated with defense expenditure. As a result, border industries and the border economy grew in concert with the government's defense appropriations and experienced industrial cycles distinct from those in the older and more traditional manufacturing centers of the Northeast and Midwest. It was perhaps natural that the states along the boundary would particularly benefit from government-stimulated industrialization, since the region's economy had been closely tied to the federal budget since the depression (and earlier, with federal support of railroad construction). World War II shifted the government's financial emphasis from primary-sector activities to newer industries. Abundant electricity, made available by such depression public-works projects as Hoover Dam, made the border states an attractive site for new war industries that required low-cost energy. Such projects as the aqueduct from the Colorado River to the southern California coastal plain and the All-American Canal to the Imperial Valley ensured the availability of water for both agriculture and growing cities.

Wartime migration to the border states fueled the economic upsurge, as people from the East and Midwest responded to the attraction of higher wages. New industries related to the war effort—particularly shipbuilding and airplane production—created a wartime employment boom and provided a foundation for continued growth after the end of the conflict. The war effort expanded the navy presence in the West, with the construction of huge bases in San Diego, San Francisco, and Los Angeles-Long Beach. The army and the marines built up large concentrations of men and matériel at Fort Bliss, Fort Ord, Travis Air Force Base, the Presidio in San Francisco, and Camp Pendleton. Some areas of the Southwest had long served as armed-forces training centers and could be quickly mobilized for the war effort. Texas, for example, rapidly became a hub of the wartime air training effort.

World War II industrialization of the border economy received added impetus from the financial accumulation of the early 1940s. In 1939, California's per capita income was still below its 1930 level, and total personal income was only 5 billion dollars. By 1945 personal income had tripled to some 15 billion dollars. That same year the state's leading financial institution, the Bank of America, held deposits and assets worth 5 billion dollars, establishing it as the world's largest bank and setting the stage for its enormous expansion in the immediate postwar years.

At the same time that the war effort sparked new economic activities, it boosted the demand for the West's traditional extractive products. The call for mineral products such as petroleum, copper, and uranium surged during the war years. Western farms became larger as the number of farms and farming families declined. In 1940, California had 133,000 farms, averaging 230 acres each. By 1985 the total had dropped to 79,000, and the average size had nearly doubled to 418 acres.[2] The war inverted farmers' longtime concern over crop surpluses into worry over shortages.

World War II also stimulated important economic changes in Mexico and in the Mexican border states. The nation embarked on a fifty-year period of radical economic transformation, industrializing on the basis of consumer goods destined for an expanding domestic market. Automobiles, tires, radios, televisions, and home appliances were among the country's new products, and foreign technology, investments, and capital were influential in developing production of the items. Mexican investors played a complementary role by establishing ancillary industries with less-complex technological requirements or by coinvesting in joint-ownership firms. The Mexican government supported industrialization by protecting the domestic market with tariffs, facilitating the import of needed capital goods, and creating the necessary infrastructure of highways, bridges, and other networks for getting products to their markets.[3]

U.S. involvement in World War II provided two crucial stimuli to Mexican industrial development: implicit protection from imports (because goods previously exported from the United States to Mexico were reserved for the war effort) and increased wartime demand (and consequent high prices) for Mexican exports. Rapidly expanding markets for Mexico's traditional exports in the decade after 1940—particularly minerals, cotton, and oil seeds—fueled a surge in foreign-exchange earnings that could not be exhausted in available imports. The Mexican Miracle of the 1950s and 1960s was established upon these pillars. The gross domestic product (GDP) more than tripled between 1940 and 1960. Mexico sustained average growth rates of 6.7 percent between 1940 and 1950, 5.8 percent between 1950 and 1960, and 6.4 percent from 1960 to 1968. The country employed 58 percent more people in the late 1960s than it had in 1940.

During and after the war the Mexican border states were incorporated into Mexico's industrial boom. Monterrey, Nuevo León, had been one of the country's leading manufacturing centers since the late nineteenth century. When the U.S. war effort blocked the city's access to many manufactured goods, local industrialists responded by investing in new production facilities; they continued to invest in the immediate aftermath of the war. Between 1945 and 1950 industrial investments increased fourfold, and the city emerged as the nation's second manufacturing center, just behind Mexico City. Local leaders founded the private Instituto Tecnológico y de Estudios Superiores de Monterrey (also known as Monterrey Tech) in order to provide technicians and engineers for the new factories; the public Universidad Autónoma de Nuevo León became one of the country's largest public universities. By 1980 more than one-half of all Mexican industrial workers in the border area were employed in Nuevo León, more than 90 percent of whom were employed in Monterrey.[4]

After 1940, agriculture, which had benefited from irrigation policies and land reform in the 1920s and 1930s, experienced increased emphasis on capital-intensive mechanized methods, large-scale irrigation works, and

greater use of pesticides and herbicides to raise productivity. One important aspect of government policy that contributed to the Mexican Miracle
was substantial outlays for agricultural infrastructure in the border states.
The impact of federal expenditure was particularly noticeable in commercial
agriculture. During the war and early postwar years the government
stepped up investments in northern irrigation and agriculture. From 1947
to 1960, 20 percent of Mexico's total expenditures for irrigation were in
Tamaulipas, 16 percent in Baja California Norte, and 25 percent in Sonora.
Dams were constructed to channel water, allowing expansion of commercial
agriculture, and the North boasted between 70 percent and 80 percent of
the newly irrigated lands. By 1970 the northern Pacific region of Mexico
accounted for 53 percent of the nation's irrigated farmland.

As a result of these wartime changes, the border states developed
Mexico's most modern, commercial, export-oriented agricultural sector.
Scientific farming boomed; the use of fertilizers and pesticides increased
yields, contributing to the North's economic prosperity. Between 1940 and
1960 the North received over 50 percent of the country's new paved roads.
Crucial to agricultural production and distribution, they created communication corridors that still exist. Private commercial holdings benefited from
federal policy to a far greater extent than did small holdings and *ejidos*,
although northern Mexico also received more than 60 percent of the total
bank loans to *ejidos*.[5] In the easternmost area of the border region, Matamoros became Mexico's most important cotton-producing region, specializing
in the processing of the fiber as well.

As California became the leading agricultural producer in the United
States (boasting one-quarter of all U.S. irrigated farmland), the agricultural complex of the Mexican North turned increasingly to the U.S. market, first for cotton, then for fruits and vegetables. The population of Mexican
border towns such as Mexicali, Reynosa, Matamoros, and Ciudad Juárez
swelled to serve the local agricultural economy as well as the tides of seasonal
farmworkers bound for Mexican fields and for the expanding agricultural
belt of the U.S. Southwest.

Arid soils on both sides of the border presented a common problem
that both countries met by supporting significant irrigation and other

TABLE 4-1
IRRIGATED LAND ON THE BORDER, 1930–1982 (THOUSANDS OF ACRES)

State	1930	1940	1950	1960	1970	1980
Baja Calif.	227	366	482	568	442	511
Chihuahua	286	336	378	558	457	299
Coahuila	612	597	674	741	494	593
Nuevo León	162	244	232	287	203	84
Sonora	285	376	692	1,371	1,561	1,398
Tamaulipas	91	131	442	785	877	963
Mexican Border	**1,663**	**2,050**	**2,900**	**4,310**	**4,034**	**3,848**

State	1930	1940	1949	1959	1969	1982
Arizona	576	576	964	1,152	1,178	1,099
California	4,745	4,277	6,438	7,396	7,249	8,460
New Mexico	527	436	655	732	823	5,573
Texas	799	895	3,123	5,656	6,888	4,241
U.S. Border	**6,647**	**6,184**	**11,180**	**14,936**	**16,138**	**15,940**

Source: Lorey, *United States-Mexico Border Statistics since 1900,* Table 1100.

infrastructure development. Table 4-1 shows the growth of irrigated lands in the ten border states from 1930 to 1982. The most rapid expansion of irrigation occurred in the depression and World War II decades, when the irrigated area almost doubled in the border region as a whole. By the 1980s the once arid land under irrigation was significantly more than twice that in 1930. Because most of the irrigation was made possible by federally funded water projects, the data indicating the amount of irrigated land provide a good gauge of the importance of federal expenditure in the region as a whole.

Roads linking the border region to Mexico's interior facilitated U.S. travel to Mexico via automobile. Between 1940 and 1960 the number of U.S. tourists crossing the border increased by more than 400 percent, from eight million to thirty-nine million. Border transactions associated with tourism accounted for 15 percent of Mexican exports of goods and services in 1940 and 27 percent by 1960. The wartime expansion of U.S. military bases along the international boundary helped boost tourism. Fort Bliss—near El Paso—grew from 3,000 soldiers in 1938 to 25,000 in 1941. A return to Prohibition in Texas during the war also stimulated crossings to Mexican border towns.

Some of the economic development of the border region in both traditional and industrial sectors during this period stemmed directly from wartime collaboration between the United States and Mexico. A bilateral commission was established to study problems requiring coordinated bilateral actions. Aided by the United States, Mexico was to maintain and intensify its production of necessary prime materials for the fabrication of munitions and other elements for the war effort. Mexico produced substantial amounts of minerals for the U.S. war machine, including copper, lead, and mercury: mercury production grew from 170 tons in 1937 to 1,117 tons in 1942. Antimony for munitions and arsenic for insecticides were also produced. In return for this aid the United States promised to make scarce machinery available to Mexico and to send technicians to help increase agricultural production. A U.S. and Mexican team also worked to help solve Mexico's transport problems. Long neglected, Mexico's railroads, upgraded with the input of U.S. expertise and rolling stock, were crucial to the transportation of goods from Mexico to the United States during the war years and afterward.[6]

Wartime cooperation was reflected in increased bilateral trade in the border region. Between 1940 and 1945, 1 million tons of goods were transshipped through border cities (the number of tons grew to 2.75 million in 1950 and 3.3 million in 1960). The increase in trade at ports of entry between 1940 and 1960 was 153 percent. The increase in Mexicali was 878 percent. These shifts had profound effects in border cities. The labor force doubled in Ciudad Juárez, as inhabitants found employment related to the rise in trade and in other sectors stimulated by the war.

With the outbreak of World War II, a new wave of migrants crossed the border from Mexico, this time under the official auspices of the U.S. government. Prompted by the immediate shortage of labor, farmers in the region pressured the federal government for permission to import temporary workers from Mexico. In 1942 the government in Washington responded with an emergency farm labor plan—the Bracero Program. Initially, the Farm Security Administration (FSA) oversaw the program, but agribusiness, which considered the FSA too pro-union and too radical, pressured the government to transfer control to the more conservative War Food Administration, where growers had more influence. The program was so successful that in April 1943 the United States and Mexico signed an agreement providing for a Bracero-type plan for importing railroad workers. Under this arrangement the United States was authorized to bring in 20,000 additional Mexican workers in 1943, 50,000 in 1944, and 75,000 in 1945.

Between 1942 and 1947 the Bracero Program brought 309,538 agricultural workers into the United States, 219,000 of them from Mexico. Fully one-half of all the Mexicans labored in California agriculture.[7] After the war the Truman administration maintained the Bracero Program in agriculture. With the outbreak of the Korean War, Congress enacted Public Law 78 in 1951, providing formal legislative recognition of a new arrangement with Mexico. Although approved as a wartime emergency measure, the law in fact established a continuing Bracero Program, first renegotiated in 1954 and then renewed regularly until 1964. In the peak year of 1957, California imported 192,438 braceros. These migrant workers were unevenly distributed among large and small farms. In 1959 a mere 5.4 percent of California farms employed 59 percent of total seasonal labor.

This wartime flow of labor north to the U.S. border states and beyond marked the beginning of the massive influx of Mexicans to both the Mexican and U.S. border states. The northward movement of inexpensive Mexican labor, beginning as an implicit subsidy to U.S. agriculture, would gradually mold the economic and social profile of the United States in the late twentieth century.[8]

Within the overall development of the border region during and after the war, California in the United States and Nuevo León, Baja California, and Chihuahua in Mexico saw the most dramatic transformation of their economies. California, which received 10 percent of all government expenditure during the war years, saw its economy boom and its population soar. At the same time, Nuevo León consolidated its position as the center of Mexico's heavy industrial development, with the expansion of facilities for steel, cement, and glass, as well as consumer-goods production. Mexican nationals in Monterrey also participated greatly in the industrialization process.

As Monterrey's industrialization gave rise to a large, urban, industrial work force, it also brought to the fore questions of labor relations. Local employers accepted neither the central government's recognition of organized labor nor its official body, the Confederación de Trabajadores de México. Instead they supported company unions, which often functioned as personnel departments of Monterrey's firms. In part because of Monterrey's influence throughout the border region, unionization, with only local exceptions, never spread broadly in the Mexican border states.

The era spanning the Great Depression and World War II left an indelible legacy throughout the border region. Considerable government spending and high-tech production in field and factory would characterize the economy of the U.S. West long after the end of the war. And the Mexican economy's wartime pattern of growth would leave a strong imprint on Mexican development in the 1950s, 1960s, and 1970s. In both Mexico and the United States the World War II years transformed the regional economies along the international boundary from economies based largely on agriculture and mining to economies based on manufacturing, technological innovation, and services. Growth was made possible by subsidized infrastructure, including—with the Bracero Program—subsidized labor costs. This trend established a long-lasting pattern in which federal expenditure and streams of migrant workers would undergird the development of both the U.S. West and the Mexican North.

NOTES

1. Martínez, *Border Boom Town,* p. 83.
2. Ellen Liebman, *California Farmland: A History of Large Agricultural Landholdings* (Totowa, NJ: Rowman and Allanheld, 1983), pp. 160–67, 169–73; U.S. Department of Commerce, Bureau of the Census, *Statistical Abstract of the United States, 1950* (Washington, DC: Government Printing Office, 1950), pp. 49, 563; U.S. Department of Commerce, Bureau of the Census, *Statistical Abstract of the United States, 1986* (Washington, DC: Government Printing Office, 1986), pp. 635, 636.

3. On the Mexican economy and U.S.-Mexican trade relations during the Second World War and in the postwar period, see Timothy King, *Mexico: Industrial and Trade Policies since 1940* (London: Oxford University Press, 1970); Niblo; René Villarreal, *El desequilibrio externo en la industrialización de México (1929–1975): Un enfoque estructuralista* (Mexico, D.F.: Fondo de Cultura Económica, 1976); Clark W. Reynolds, *The Mexican Economy: Twentieth-Century Structure and Growth* (New Haven: Yale University Press, 1970); and Leopoldo M. Solís, *La realidad económica mexicana: Retrovisión y perspectivas* (Mexico, D.F.: Siglo Veintiuno Editores, 1987).

4. Menno Vellinga, *Desigualdad, poder y cambio social en Monterrey* (Mexico, D.F.: Siglo Veintiuno Editores, 1988), p. 42.

5. Reynolds, *The Mexican Economy*, p. 158.

6. Stephen R. Niblo, *War, Diplomacy, and Development: The United States and Mexico, 1938–1954* (Wilmington: Scholarly Resources, 1995).

7. On the Bracero Program, see Ernesto Galarza, *Merchants of Labor: The Mexican Bracero Program* (Charlotte, NC: McNally and Loftin, 1964); Richard Craig, *The Bracero Program: Interest Groups and Foreign Policy* (Austin: University of Texas Press, 1971); Linda C. Majka and Theo J. Majka, *Farm Workers, Agribusiness, and the State* (Philadelphia: Temple University Press, 1982); Rodolfo Acuña, *Occupied America: A History of Chicanos,* 2d ed. (New York: Harper and Row, 1981).

8. For the classic historical account of these beginnings, see Carey McWilliams, *North from Mexico: The Spanish-Speaking People of the United States* (New York: Greenwood Press, 1968).

| # ECONOMIC TRENDS SINCE 1950

LEGACIES OF THE WARTIME ECONOMY

THE ECONOMIC SIGNIFICANCE of the border region for both the United States and Mexico increased dramatically after 1950. After the boom caused by the expanded demand of the war effort, the economy on both sides of the border settled into a prolonged period of sustained growth, the first in its history. New economic pursuits and the stability brought by the increasing diversity of the economic base undergirded this transformed pattern of development. The federal governments in both Mexico and the United States continued to stimulate border economic development by investing in infrastructure. This was particularly the case in the U.S. West, where "the rising federal role as regional financier–resources manager, which had begun so abruptly in 1933–45, was heightened, expanded, and institutionalized."[1] By the end of the century, as the region as a whole became caught up in the world economy's momentous shift from an Atlantic to a Pacific axis, the border's economy emerged as the focus of scholarly attention, debate among policymakers, and increasing general interest.

THE BORDER ECONOMY COMES OF AGE

Economic trends established during World War II continued into the 1950s, becoming, if anything, more pronounced in peacetime. In the decade and a half following the end of the war, the U.S. federal government invested an additional 150 billion dollars in the U.S. West, most of it in the four border states. Texas and California benefited from federal spending through defense contracts, price supports for farm commodities, and generous outlays for veterans. San Antonio, like San Diego, developed a postwar economy heavily dependent on the military. Los Alamos, New Mexico, continued as a major center of federally funded nuclear research.

Throughout the postwar period, expenditures for defense constituted the largest single item in the federal budget, a national priority that had a profound impact on the border region. Defense-related production, most of which was financed by the federal government, continued to lead the border's industrial development. Federal support of high-tech industries also characterized the period after 1950. Government financing of high-risk research and development helped provide a competitive edge to U.S. industries. The importance of military spending was felt well into the 1980s. In 1984, California led all states in garnering federal military dollars, with 20 percent (nearly 40 billion dollars) of the total allocation. Of the funds set aside for military contracts, the state's producers received 23 percent, or 28.5 billion dollars of the U.S. total. The country's active-duty military personnel, 15 percent of whom were stationed in California, also contributed to numerous local economies.

The postwar federal budget never returned to prewar levels. Firms such as Lockheed, McDonnell-Douglas, Rockwell International, Motorola, Sperry Corporation, Hughes Aircraft, General Dynamics, and, later, Texas Instruments took advantage of government largesse to become leaders in the new U.S. economy. The border area gained some of the country's most technologically sophisticated firms. Many aerospace, computer, and communications industries were established in or relocated to Silicon Valley in northern California (the area of the San Francisco Peninsula that stretches from Menlo Park to San Jose), as well as in Los Angeles, Phoenix,

San Diego, San Jose, Houston, Austin, and the Dallas-Fort Worth area. Although federal underwriting of western development shifted its focus from providing inexpensive land and water to building freeway networks and financing aerospace and high-tech research and development, government support continued uninterrupted.

In Mexico in the postwar period the pattern of development initiated during the war years also deepened. Mexican federal investment in the border states, which stimulated growth and contributed to changing patterns of employment, remained one of the main pillars of border development in the country after 1950. Postwar budgets for communications and public works, which had averaged 13 percent under Cárdenas in the 1930s, hovered between 18 and 23 percent.

The period after 1950 saw remarkable changes in the size and shape of state economies all along the U.S.-Mexican border. Data on the evolution of gross state product—the total value of all goods and services produced (see Tables 5-1 and 5-2)—reveal impressive absolute growth in both the United States and Mexico. The structure of regional production changed markedly over the course of the postwar period, as figures for the economically active population in different sectors of the ten border states show (see Tables 5-3 and 5-4). By 1990 only about 14 percent of Mexicans in border states were working in agriculture; fully one-quarter were employed in the industries and another one-quarter in services. In the United States the shift away from primary activities was even more impressive: in 1980 only 3.1 percent of the economically active population worked in agriculture, forestry, and fisheries, while one-fifth were employed in the industries and almost one-third worked in services.

Agriculture boomed on both sides of the border in the postwar period, as large capital-intensive farms benefited from massive investment in irrigation works. From 1947 to 1960, 20 percent of Mexico's total expenditures for irrigation were devoted to Tamaulipas, 16 percent to Baja California Norte, and 25 percent to Sonora. While Tijuana was growing as the center of the West Coast industrial hub in Mexico, Mexicali prospered from major expansion of irrigation and mechanized agriculture linked to the U.S. market. The area around Mexicali became one of Mexico's most productive

TABLE 5-1

MEXICAN BORDER-STATE GROSS PRODUCT, BY ECONOMIC SECTOR, 1970 AND 1985

	1970		1985	
	Border	Mexico	Border	Mexico
Total gross product (millions of current pesos)	93,714	444,271	8,787,037	47,402,549
Sector	Percent of Total			
Agriculture	12.7	12.2	9.6	9.1
Mining	3.5	2.5	2.4	4.7
Manufacturing	21.6	23.7	25.7	23.4
Construction	6.0	5.3	4.8	4.4
Trade, restaurants, and hotels	28.0	25.9	32.6	34.8
Utilities	1.2	1.2	1.3	0.8
Services	22.0	24.4	23.6	22.8

Source: Lorey, *United States-Mexico Border Statistics since 1900*, Table 52.

TABLE 5-2

U.S. BORDER-STATE GROSS PRODUCT, BY ECONOMIC SECTOR, 1963–1985

	1963	1972	1982	1985
Total gross product (millions of dollars)	103,027	213,940	680,675	876,941
Sector	Percent of Total			
Farms	3.4	2.5	2.0	1.7
Agricultural services, forestry, and fisheries	0.4	0.6	0.6	0.5
Mining	5.0	3.4	8.3	5.9
Construction	5.5	5.4	5.0	5.1
Manufacturing	20.5	18.2	17.3	17.2
Durable goods	(12.1)	(10.8)	(10.7)	(10.9)
Nondurable goods	(8.4)	(7.4)	(6.6)	(6.3)
Transportation and public utilities	9.2	9.0	8.7	9.0
Wholesale trade	6.7	7.0	7.0	7.2
Retail trade	10.3	10.4	9.6	10.0
Finance, insurance, and real estate	15.1	16.2	14.6	15.2
Services	11.7	13.1	15.4	16.8
Federal government	2.4	2.9	2.1	2.1
Military	2.5	2.7	1.8	1.7
State and local government	7.2	8.6	7.5	7.6

Source: Lorey, *United States-Mexico Border Statistics since 1900*, Table 1605.

TABLE 5-3
MEXICAN BORDER-STATE ECONOMICALLY ACTIVE POPULATION,
BY ECONOMIC SECTOR, 1970–1990

Sector	1970 (%)	1980 (%)	1990 (%)
Primary activities	29.1	15.4	14.3
Extractive industry	2.4	0.7	1.6
Manufacturing	17.4	15.2	24.1
Construction	5.8	6.7	8.4
Electricity and water	0.4	0.3	0.8
Commerce	11.7	11.1	14.0
Transportation	3.7	4.6	4.8
Services	20.6	17.0	25.1
Government	3.0	—	3.6
Unclassified	5.8	29.0	3.2

Source: Lorey, *United States-Mexico Border Statistics since 1900,* Table 701.

agricultural regions and attracted numerous national and international manufacturing concerns as well.

The four U.S. border states together came to account for one-fifth of U.S. farm production.[2] After 1949, California remained consistently the nation's number-one agricultural state in cash income, and by 1989 it accounted for 13 percent of total U.S. farm production. By 1960, Mexico's northern region was producing 44 percent of the gross value of agriculture,

TABLE 5-4
U.S. BORDER-STATE EMPLOYED PERSONS, BY ECONOMIC SECTOR, 1970 AND 1980

Sector	1970 (%)	1980 (%)
Agriculture, forestry, and fisheries	3.7	3.1
Mining	1.3	1.7
Construction	6.3	6.9
Manufacturing	19.9	18.7
Transportation, communication, and public utilities	7.0	7.2
Wholesale trade	4.5	4.6
Retail trade	17.0	16.6
Finance, insurance, and real estate	5.6	6.7
Services	28.5	29.4
Public administration	6.2	5.1

Source: Lorey, *United States-Mexico Border Statistics since 1900,* Table 702.

livestock, fishery, and forestry production in Mexico.[3] The four Mexican border states depended more on farm production than did Mexico as a whole. Whereas agriculture accounted for 8 percent of Mexico's GDP in 1980, it represented 17 percent of the gross state product in Sonora, 12 percent in Tamaulipas, 12 percent in Chihuahua, and 9 percent in Baja California Norte.

In both the Mexican and the U.S. border states, the agricultural boom was accompanied by a progressive concentration of farmlands, as family farms gave way to large, vertically integrated agribusinesses. By the 1970s, it is estimated, 70 percent of *ejidos* in Sonora rented their lands to private producers. The most dynamic sectors in Mexican border agriculture were increasingly geared toward the cultivation of fruit and vegetables for export to the United States during the winter months. In the period from 1960 to 1983 the Mexican border states also experienced striking growth in the production of animal-feed grains.

Manufacturing was increasingly a mainstay of the U.S.-Mexican border economy after 1950. In the U.S. border states clean industry led the way after the 1960s, as is evidenced by the data in Table 5-5, which ranks, in order of value added, the primary branches of manufacturing in the 1980s. Mexican industry was more concentrated in such basic industrial sectors as food processing and mineral refining. Production was concentrated geographically. By the mid-1980s, Los Angeles was the most important manufacturing center in the United States. Together the Monterrey industrial conglomerates—controlled by a small clique of interconnected families— were responsible for about one-quarter of Mexico's industrial output. By the mid-1950s the Mexican North generated most of the country's industrial production outside of central Mexico: of the nation's twenty-five leading industrial centers, seventeen were northern cities.

Highly specialized links between the two national economies in the border region were particularly striking in such areas as the industrial corridor between San Antonio, Texas, and Monterrey, Nuevo León. In Monterrey, factories and assembly plants combined U.S. capital goods and high-tech know-how with Mexican production skill and inexpensive labor. Monterrey was the origin of 60 percent of all manufactured goods

TABLE 5-5
THREE PRIMARY BRANCHES OF MANUFACTURING IN MEXICO (1980)
AND IN THE UNITED STATES (1982), BY STATE

State	Branches of Manufacturing
Baja California	Food and allied products Beverages Nonmetallic minerals
Chihuahua	Mining and refining Electric and electronic equipment Lumber and wood products
Coahuila	Primary metals Machinery, except electrical Electric and electronic equipment
Nuevo León	Primary metals Nonmetallic minerals Chemicals and allied products
Sonora	Nonferrous minerals Food and allied products Electric and electronic equipment
Tamaulipas	Chemicals and allied products Electric and electronic equipment Food and allied products
Arizona	Electric and electronic equipment Machinery, except electrical Transportation equipment
California	Printing and publishing Electric and electronic equipment Transportation equipment
New Mexico	Petroleum and coal products Electric and electronic equipment Food and allied products
Texas	Machinery, except electrical Chemicals and allied products Food and allied products

Source: Lorey, *United States-Mexico Border Statistics since 1900,* Tables 1400 and 1401.

entering the United States from Mexico. North of the border, San Antonio was a top distribution center and supplier of U.S. services to manufacturers in Monterrey. Law firms and accounting firms opened offices in San Antonio to serve the growing Mexican market.

When older U.S. industries such as textiles, automobiles, and steel began to suffer from slow growth and increased foreign competition in the 1960s and 1970s, the newer high-tech firms continued to be buoyant. Often located in the Southwest, they helped the region's economy remain relatively strong through the 1970s and 1980s. By the 1980s the United States exported only a small amount of steel; aerospace products and computer equipment—produced predominantly in border states—became the nation's leading exports. With many of the new firms in the border area, the four states north of the international boundary together outperformed the rest of the U.S. industrial economy after 1970. These industries developed in close relationship with the Pentagon's priorities and were built upon the high-tech industrial base already well established in the border states. Largely because of Silicon Valley—one of the leading sites of the emerging computer,

TABLE 5-6
PERCENTAGE OF MEXICAN-ORIGIN POPULATION IN THE UNITED STATES, EMPLOYED IN INDUSTRY, BY IMMIGRANT STATUS AND SEX, 1980

| | *Males* | | *Females* | |
| | *Immigrant Status* | | *Immigrant Status* | |
Industry	*I*[a]	*II*[b]	*I*[a]	*II*[b]
Agriculture, mining	17.3	9.0	10.4	4.0
Construction	11.1	13.0	0.6	0.9
Manufacturing	35.3	23.7	44.5	19.2
Transportation, communication, and utilities	2.4	9.3	1.0	3.7
Wholesaling and nonfood retailing	8.7	12.9	8.4	13.5
Food retailing	12.2	7.1	8.0	11.0
Business, repair, personal services	8.7	7.7	15.3	10.8
Professional services, finance, public administration	4.3	17.4	11.8	37.0

Source: Lorey, *United States-Mexico Border Statistics since 1900*, Table 1009.
[a] Mexican-born noncitizens who immigrated to the United States in 1975 or later.
[b] Persons born in the United States who identify themselves as being of Mexican origin.

communications, and software industrial complex—the border states continued to lead the nation in high-tech products, processes, services, and exports.[4] The trend toward high-tech production was also notable in Baja California and Chihuahua. Electronic and computer industries often drove the border economy in a symbiotic manner, with innovation taking place in the United States and assembly carried out in Mexico.

Both U.S. citizens of Mexican descent and undocumented Mexican immigrants played a major part in the postwar economic boom on the border, particularly in the growth of the manufacturing and service sectors. Data on the occupations of Mexican immigrants show that more than one-third of the men who arrived after 1975 and about 45 percent of the women were employed in manufacturing in 1980 (see Table 5-6), a marked change from the years of the Bracero Program. Data on the employers of undocumented workers in the United States (see Table 5-7) reveal that recent immigrants

TABLE 5-7

MAJOR U.S. EMPLOYERS OF UNDOCUMENTED WORKERS, 1980

Industry	Percentage of Undocumented Workers	Industry	Percentage of Undocumented Workers
Apparel	10.59	Meat products	1.40
Eating and drinking		Retail grocers	1.40
establishments	7.39	Primary metals	1.39
Construction	6.46	Wholesale grocers	1.33
Crop farming	6.46	Chemicals and allied products	1.26
Electrical machinery	3.06	Rubber and plastics	1.26
Fabricated metals	2.53	Real estate and services to dwellings	1.20
Transportation equipment	2.40	Auto repair	1.00
Educational institutions	2.26	Lumber and wood products	1.00
Miscellaneous manufacturing	2.26	Paper and allied products	1.00
Grain and bakery products	2.03	Cleaners	0.93
Motels and hotels	1.93	Horticulture	0.93
Furniture and fixtures	1.86	Agricultural services	0.87
Private households	1.80	Beverages and miscellaneous	
Canned fruits and vegetables	1.79	food products	0.83
Leather and footwear	1.66	Department stores	0.80
Textiles	1.66	Electronic computing equipment	0.73
Hospitals	1.53	Other	25.00

Source: Lorey, *United States-Mexico Border Statistics since 1900,* Table 724.

were concentrated in some of the lowest-paying and least-secure sectors: apparel manufacture, restaurants, agriculture, and construction.

On both sides of the border some of the most traditional economic pursuits fell into permanent decline and stagnation in the years after 1960. The most important traditional sector to experience a long-term slump was copper, silver, and gold mining. At one time the lifeblood of the border states, the extraction of almost all minerals decreased in importance after a short-lived boom in the 1950s, while the ownership of mining operations became increasingly concentrated. A few states remained leading national and international sources of important metals and minerals. The state of Chihuahua, for example, continued to produce quantities of lead, silver, gold, copper, and fluorite, while Coahuila became an important source of coal for the nearby steel factories in Monclova and Monterrey. Tamaulipas possessed little of Mexico's traditional mineral wealth but served, into the 1970s, as one of the main centers of the country's oil industry. The states of Texas and Tamaulipas sat atop the same oil reserves and shared the booms and busts of that industry. In the 1940s and 1950s, discoveries of natural gas near Reynosa provided added wealth for Tamaulipas.[5] Sonora and Arizona continued to be important sources of copper.

Tourism, another traditional activity of the border region, which had touched off or contributed to economic booms during Prohibition and World War II, continued as one of the mainstays of the border economy after 1950. Tourism was important on both sides of the boundary: a great majority of Mexican tourists journeyed to the U.S. border states, and the number of tourists traveling from U.S. border states to Mexico grew twenty-fourfold between 1935 and 1970. Most went to Mexico to indulge in such traditional pursuits as entertainment (principally food and drink) and bargain hunting (apparel and personal-care items). Tourism was the greatest source of foreign exchange in Tijuana and in several other border cities.[6] Border commerce typically experienced periodic downturns, however. Retail sales to Mexican shoppers on the U.S. side of the border were extremely sensitive to fluctuations in the dollar-peso exchange rate, plunging dramatically with each major postwar devaluation of the Mexican peso (1976, 1982, 1985, 1994–95). After the Mexican crisis of 1982, U.S. border merchants sought federal assistance, and President Ronald Reagan responded by creating a Border Aid Program. Along with tourism, a wide range of services—law, finance, health, entertainment, education, and transportation, to name a few—began to employ large segments of the U.S. and Mexican border-state work force.

MEXICAN GOVERNMENT POLICY
AND THE BORDER:
PRONAF AND BIP—THE *MAQUILADORAS*

Beginning in the 1960s the Mexican federal government played an increasingly active role in managing the economic growth of the country's North. This change came with the massive transformation of the region as its population grew. Also involved was the desire to secure income (by ensuring that money would be spent on the Mexican rather than the U.S. side of the border), to provide for the absorption of excess labor in the region, and to attract family tourism as vice-based tourism waned.

Mexican government policy reflected changes in global production as well, particularly shifts in the United States. As goods produced in Europe and Asia began to flood the U.S. market, the value of imports as a share of U.S. domestic production rose from 14 percent to 40 percent (in the 1970–1979 period). Mexican policymakers' desire to compete with these imports was aided by a new U.S. tariff law in 1965, which exempted from general import duties U.S. goods assembled in whole or in part outside the United States. With a tariff to be paid only on value added in manufacture, in many cases it became cheaper to have goods assembled abroad and import them than to produce or assemble them in the United States. Most U.S. foreign investment in Mexico prior to the 1960s had been in extractive industries, but in the 1970s U.S. factories began to shift assembly and even some production to Mexico.

In 1961, Mexico established a national border program, the Programa Nacional Fronterizo (PRONAF). Under the auspices of the publicly owned national development bank NAFINSA, PRONAF sought to substitute Mexican manufactured goods for imports in the border states, boost the sale of Mexican manufactures to foreign consumers, stimulate tourism in the border states, and upgrade living conditions along the boundary.

The program was most successful in the area of commerce. By the mid-1960s the number of Mexicans shopping on the U.S. side of the border had begun to grow dramatically, outpacing the number of U.S. citizens who shopped south of the border. Studies indicated that 70 percent of Juarenses visited El Paso to shop, their expenditures on food, clothing, and furniture constituting 62 percent of the total spent on these items in El Paso. This trend revealed the inadequate commercial infrastructure of cities like Ciudad Juárez. In response, PRONAF supported the construction of such shopping complexes as Rio Grande Mall in Ciudad Juárez, where shoppers could find both Mexican-made and U.S. and other foreign goods. In a further, controversial, effort to strengthen Mexican retailing, streetcar service between Ciudad Juárez and El Paso was discontinued in 1977.

Mexican government policy received an unexpected boost when the 1976 devaluation of the peso stimulated the sale of Mexican goods and services to U.S. consumers. The devaluation also triggered a boom in U.S. tourism, as travelers took advantage of a strengthened dollar. The same year saw an 80 percent increase in vehicular flow between El Paso and Ciudad Juárez; at the end of 1976, commerce in Ciudad Juárez had increased 60 percent over 1975. The devaluation was calamitous for El Paso merchants, however, who had grown to depend on Mexican pesos and shoppers. Some store owners in the downtown area experienced a 50 percent drop in sales.

The Mexican government established a Border Industrialization Program (BIP) in 1965 with the twin goals of stimulating the manufacturing sector of the depressed economies in the northern states and providing employment for workers displaced by the end of the Bracero program in 1964. The BIP was also established to respond to changes in the world economy. As flexible inter- and intrafirm networks developed to provide on-time deliveries and carefully managed quality control, Mexico became a more attractive location for assembly operations for the neighboring U.S. market. In addition, new communications technologies made it possible for firms to carry out production efficiently at diverse world sites.[7]

Flags of Japan, Mexico, and the United States fly over a Tijuana *maquiladora*.
Paul Ganster, Institute for Regional Studies of the Californias

The main feature of the border industrialization program was the establishment of *maquilas* or *maquiladoras*, assembly plants that imported components and raw goods from the United States, assembled them into finished products, and then exported them back across the border for sale. The phenomenon was sometimes called in-bond industry because the components and machinery were brought in under a bonded status that prohibited their sale in Mexico and mandated their reexport for sale abroad. In some ways the *maquiladora* program represented the logical extension of Mexico's earlier free-trade zone. Just as the free-trade zone recognized that people in the border cities needed preferential access to the U.S. market, the *maquiladora* program recognized the special importance of the U.S. market for Mexican industrial development.[8] The *maquila* innovation was developed at roughly the same time as, and at least in part as a response to, the emergence of the Export Processing Zones and Special Economic Zones of Asia.

The attractions of *maquila* operations for U.S. and Asian investors were several. The enabling legislation provided for the duty-free importation of materials, supplies, and machinery as long as the whole of the product was for export; tariffs were paid solely on the value added by manufacture in Mexico, generating a substantial savings. *Maquilas* were also the only firms exempt from the Mexican laws requiring majority Mexican ownership. Producers could take advantage of the proximity of advanced transportation infrastructure on the U.S. side. Labor organization was less entrenched in the Mexican border cities than in either the United States or central Mexico. Few strikes were threatened or carried out in border-state manufacturing plants. For these reasons the *maquila* plants came to constitute an increasingly important link in the booming intra-industry trade reshaping global investment and commercial flows. In contrast with

The *maquilas* provided an almost constant demand for assemblers.
David E. Lorey

other global locations, the area offered managers the advantage of living on the U.S. side, where families had access to U.S. schools, health care, and other public services.

The *maquiladora* program gathered steam slowly at first. Between 1965 and the mid-1970s a gradual rise in investments in *maquilas* in Tijuana, Mexicali, Nogales, Ciudad Juárez, and Matamoros gave rise to twin plants: labor-intensive work carried out on the Mexican side, capital- and development-intensive on the U.S. side. Even with a sluggish start, by 1972 nearly one-third of the value of all U.S. components sent abroad for assembly was going to border plants in Mexico. After 1972, *maquilas* were no longer legally limited to the border region. Although 80 percent were still concentrated in the border states, and almost all of that activity took place in five cities along the border, *maquilas* spread slowly to other areas, notably Guadalajara. An overvalued Mexican peso led to job losses in the *maquiladoras* in the mid-1970s; the industry gradually recovered until 1983. By 1979, *maquiladora* production accounted for one-quarter of Mexico's manufacturing exports. With the Mexican national economic crisis of the early 1980s, the *maquiladora* program became a crucial part of the government's economic strategy to attract foreign capital to Mexican manufacturing.

The number of border *maquila* plants and the number of workers they employed grew rapidly after the early 1980s (see Table 5-8). From a total of twelve plants in 1965, *maquila* operations multiplied to twenty-two hundred by 1996; the number of employees increased from 3,000 to almost 700,000 in the same period. The majority of the plants were concentrated in Tijuana and Ciudad Juárez, some in formal industrial parks. Although only 1 percent of Mexico's economically active population worked in border *maquiladora* plants, these workers constituted more than one in every ten Mexicans in manufacturing jobs. It was estimated that by the turn of the century, border assembly plants would employ well over a million workers.

Maquilas produced a wide variety of goods for export to the United States, including electric and electronic goods, clothing, transportation equipment, furniture, toys, and processed foods (see Table 5-9). By the early 1980s the majority of television sets, refrigerators, and computer keyboards sold

TABLE 5-8
NUMBER OF *MAQUILADORA* EMPLOYEES
IN TOP SIX BORDER MUNICIPALITIES, 1975–1995

Municipality	1975	1980	1985	1990	1995
Ciudad Juárez	19,775	39,402	77,592	122,231	155,422
Nuevo Laredo	1,928	2,462	3,603	14,747	—
Matamoros	9,778	15,231	20,686	38,361	43,553
Mexicali	6,324	7,146	10,876	20,729	24,965
Reynosa	1,255	5,450	12,761	24,801	41,466
Tijuana	7,844	12,343	25,913	59,871	93,557
Total in Mexico	67,214	119,546	211,968	446,436	639,979

Source: Lorey, *United States-Mexico Border Statistics since 1900*, Table 715.

in the United States were assembled in border *maquiladoras*. Imports to the United States from *maquilas* grew from 9 percent of total U.S. imports in 1979 to 17 percent in 1987. Soon European, Japanese, Taiwanese, and South Korean investors joined U.S. and Mexican entrepreneurs in establishing border industries under the *maquiladora* program.[9]

It turned out to be beneficial to the national economy to have *maquilas* in times of crisis—particularly in 1982 and 1995. As Mexico's 1980s economic crisis deepened, the number of *maquilas* grew, and the number of *maquila* workers increased significantly. During the 1995 decline the *maquiladora* industry expanded by at least 20 percent. In that year *maquilas* produced 5 billion dollars in exports, accounting for almost 70 percent of Mexico's trade surplus with the United States. Because statistics on Mexican exports include *maquila* production, they are sometimes misleading. One-half of the annual imports and exports claimed by the Mexican government in 1995, for example, came from the dollar-denominated, foreign-owned assembly plants.

More companies moved plants south of the border in the 1980s, transforming even towns at some distance from the international boundary. One example was Cananea (the mining town whose 1906 eruption had seemed to many a precursor of the Mexican Revolution of 1910), where several large *maquiladoras* opened, attracting workers from the interior of Sonora and from surrounding states. After 1983 *maquilas* were allowed to sell 20 percent of their production in Mexico; in 1989 this amount was

TABLE 5-9

MAQUILADORA GOODS PRODUCED IN BORDER MUNICIPALITIES, BY TYPE, 1980–1990

	1980	*1985*	*1990*
Number of *Maquiladoras*	551	672	1,477
Type of Goods		*Percentage Share*	
Prepared foods	2.2	1.8	2.2
Clothes and textiles	17.1	12.1	11.2
Shoes and leather goods	3.3	4.8	2.8
Furniture	10.2	11.0	17.1
Chemical products	0.7	—	4.7
Transportation equipment	9.1	8.0	8.3
Tools and equipment	2.9	3.1	2.3
Electric and electronic equipment	11.4	10.9	5.9
Electric and electronic materials and accessories	24.9	26.3	24.0
Toys and sports materials	3.8	3.9	2.0
Other manufactures	9.6	12.8	14.9
Services	4.9	5.1	4.6

Source: Lorey, *United States-Mexico Border Statistics since 1900,* Table 1502.

increased to 50 percent. Under NAFTA, firms will eventually be able to sell any portion of their production, duty free, in any North American domestic market.

Since the *maquiladoras* were foreign-owned firms, their principal local impact was on employment and wages. *Maquila* wages, although low by average manufacturing standards in the United States (about three dollars a day in the late 1980s), were 25 percent higher than in other regions of Mexico. Because low pay was the key to their success, *maquila* owners struggled to keep unions out of the plants. Some firms preferred to employ young, female workers, considering them less likely to organize. Managers argued that women were more efficient than men at most assembly tasks that required manual dexterity and close eye-hand coordination. The preference for women workers may have unintentionally encouraged the male labor force to seek employment opportunities on the other side of the border, stimulating both legal and illegal migration to the United States. A program that had been touted as an answer to illegal migration may thus have added to it. Although women remained in the majority in the *maquiladora* work force, the ratio changed over time; by

1988, for example, men constituted 41 percent of the assembly-plant work force in Baja California.[10]

The consequences of *maquila*-led economic development of the northern Mexican states were much debated, both in Mexico and in the United States. As discussion of the implementation of a free-trade agreement between the United States and Mexico intensified in the early 1990s, the fear that Mexico would become a "*maquiladora* country" were voiced. Critics charged that *maquila* production constituted a U.S. enclave on Mexican soil, that the basis of the industry in low-wage labor indicated hyperexploitation of Mexican nationals in the interest of the U.S. consumer, and that the *maquiladoras* brought little long-term benefit to Mexican industrial infrastructure through the transfer of technology. The impact of *maquiladoras* on the environment and on the health of workers also caused concern among some observers.[11] One critic pointed out that the social infrastructure remained underdeveloped in Mexican border cities, while the U.S. government received enormous revenues from taxes on goods produced in *maquilas* by U.S. firms (businesses that were taxed at their home location in the United States). The revenues did not make their way back to the border region.[12] Labor experts noted that, until 1998, none of the *maquiladora* plants was represented by an independent workers' union; even the single, short-lived exception at a Hyundai plant in Tijuana in 1998 served to prove the general rule. In January 1998 the U.S. Labor Department—in response to a complaint filed under NAFTA rules—reported that thousands of *maquilas* administered tests to weed out pregnant applicants for assembly jobs and harassed pregnant workers to coerce their resignation.[13]

Early worries that the *maquilas* were "runaway" assembly plants that would move on at the earliest sign of lower-cost or less troublesome labor elsewhere, leaving little benefit for Mexico, proved unfounded: the assembly plants expanded their operations and appeared to be on the border to stay. Accompanying the growth in the number of *maquilas* was a reorientation of the industry: more and more *maquiladora* plants expanded from assembly operations to full-scale manufacturing, bringing significant wage and technological benefits. The industry also became more

Women assemble audiocassettes inside a Mexicali *maquila*.
Paul Ganster, Institute for Regional Studies of the Californias

diverse. Even agricultural enterprises began to use the *maquila* option to export such products as houseplants and onion powder to U.S. markets.[14] Even though NAFTA significantly altered the legal status of *maquiladora* exports, *maquila*-like assembly for the U.S. market was bound to characterize the industrial development of the Mexican border states for some time.

Some criticisms remained valid, however. By far the most serious was that *maquila* operations did not, on the whole, create backward and forward linkages as hoped. The Mexican companies that policymakers had expected would supply parts and supporting services did not emerge in large numbers. The average Mexican share of inputs was about 1.5 percent, even though that figure rose to almost 20 percent in plants proximate to Monterrey. Problems with quality, price, and delivery time plagued potential Mexican suppliers. Particularly in the border states the *maquilas* were largely enclaves that did not lead automatically to significant technological innovations in Mexican industry. The most sophisticated aspects

The border at Tijuana.
Paul Ganster, Institute for Regional Studies of the Californias

of production—including research and development—continued to be carried out in the home country and had little effect on Mexico.

Along with the creation of the *maquila* program, other political measures created an economic life on the border distinct from that in the interior of the country. In 1971, President Luis Echeverría modified the law enabling businesses on the border to import some consumer goods so that local residents would not have to do their shopping in the United States.[15] Mexican law permitted residents in border municipalities outside the free-trade zone to import small quantities of consumer goods (*artículos ganchos*) for resale, as an exception to standard customs regulations. Under this program, consumers could buy, duty-free, eighty articles that could not be manufactured in Mexico as inexpensively as in the United States. Allowing Mexican merchants to buy goods at wholesale prices in the United States and import them freely was intended to stimulate retail sales on the Mexican side of the border. The program was such a success that the Mexican government eventually generalized it to all of the border states.

The slowing of the U.S. economy after 1969 affected the border states in a number of different ways. U.S. growth rates during the 1970s were the most sluggish that they had been since the 1930s; meanwhile, inflation surged. From 1973 to 1981 world oil prices rose dramatically, lifting the Texas economy to new heights but causing other border states to experience industrial decline and unemployment between mid-1981 and 1983. International oil prices began to slide in 1982 and then nose-dived in 1986. Throughout the 1980s, Texas banks and savings and loans suffered severely from inflated real estate investment made during the earlier boom. The crisis of the 1980s caused price deflation in real estate, which led much of the financial sector into bankruptcy.[16] By the late 1980s and early 1990s the Texas boom-and-bust cycle began repeating itself nationally and then throughout the border states. Some of the symptoms were the same—overinvestment in inflated real estate markets and overproduction of domestic goods for a public determined to buy foreign products.

The coup de grâce for the U.S. border states came with the economic and political collapse of the Soviet Union after 1989, which, in turn, led to massive cuts in federal spending in the United States. Just as the West generally and border states in particular had benefited from war-related federal spending, they now reeled from the ripple effect of reduced defense expenditures and other shifts in the economy.[17] Even California's famously diverse economy proved unable to rise above the tide.

Unemployment in the four border states climbed from 5.7 percent in 1989 to 7.2 percent by the end of 1991. In California the rate of unemployment hit 7.4 percent, second only to Arizona's 7.7 percent, and by April 1992 it had risen to 8 percent, seventh in the nation (tied with Louisiana and Mississippi) and first in the U.S. border states. Not surprisingly, by September 1992, California led the four border states once again, with borrowers behind in payments or bank foreclosures on 8.5 percent of its real estate loans.[18] By the mid-1990s the bust appeared to be waning, and the California economy accelerated quickly after 1997.

It is clear that after World War II a true border economy emerged, reflecting a boundary that united rather than divided. With government initiatives, including the establishment of the *maquiladora* program, the economy of the Mexican North became increasingly tied to that of the U.S. Southwest. In the late 1990s, Mexico was second only to Canada as a U.S. trading partner. This change in the relationship between the two countries was articulated most clearly at the U.S.-Mexican border, as the region found itself at the center of the economic elements of the bilateral relationship. By the 1990s the border was no longer a line surveyed through scattered outposts of traditional economic pursuits, as it had been in 1900; instead it was a sensitive membrane of utmost importance for the economies of both the United States and Mexico, a permeable barrier through which goods and services were exchanged at an ever increasing rate.

NOTES

1. Michael T. Malone and Richard W. Etulain, *The American West: A Twentieth-Century History* (Lincoln: University of Nebraska Press, 1989), p. 262.
2. U.S. Department of Commerce, Bureau of the Census, *Statistical Abstract of the United States, 1991* (Washington, DC: Government Printing Office, 1991), p. 655.
3. Martínez, *Border Boom Town*, p. 95.
4. Roger Miller and Marcel Cáte, *Growing the Next Silicon Valley: A Guide for Successful Regional Planning* (Lexington, MA: Lexington Books, 1987), pp. 16, 27;

Arizona Office of Economic Planning and Development, *High Technology in Arizona: A Market Analysis of Suppliers in Arizona and the Southwest* (Phoenix: Arizona Office of Economic Planning and Development, 1984), pp. 8–15; Annalee Saxenian, "Silicon Valley and Route 128: Regional Prototypes or Historic Exceptions?" in *High Technology, Space, and Society,* ed. Manuel Castells (Beverly Hills: Sage Publications, 1985), pp. 82–93, 99; Ann R. Markusen and Robin Bloch, "Defensive Cities: Military Spending, High Technology, and Human Settlement," in Castells, *High Technology, Space, and Society,* pp. 106–20.

5. Juan Fidel Zorrilla and Manuel Ignacio Salinas Domíngues, "Tamaulipas," in *Visión histórica de la frontera norte de México,* ed. David Piñera Ramírez, 3 vols. (Mexicali: Universidad Autónoma de Baja California, Centro de Investigaciones Históricas, UNAM-UABC, 1987), 3:321.

6. Paul Ganster and Alan Sweedler, "The United States-Mexico Border Region: Security and Interdependence," in Lorey, *United States-Mexico Border Statistics since 1900,* p. 437.

7. See Sam Dillon, "A Twenty-Year G.M. Parts Migration to Mexico," *New York Times,* June 24, 1998.

8. Jesús Tamayo and José Luis Fernández, *Zonas fronterizas (México-Estados Unidos)* (Mexico, D.F.: Centro de Investigación y Docencia Económicas, 1983), p. 71.

9. James D. Cockcroft, *Outlaws in the Promised Land: Mexican Immigrant Workers and America's Future* (New York: Grove Press, 1986), p. 109; Dalia Barrera Bassols, *Condiciones de vida de los trabajadores de Tijuana, 1970–1978* (Mexico, D.F.: Instituto Nacional de Antropología e Historia, 1987), Table 11; Fernández-Kelly, *For We Are Sold,* p. 192.

10. Instituto Nacional de Estadística, Geografía e Informática, *Estadística de la industria maquiladora de exportación, 1975–1984* (Mexico, D.F.: Institutio Nacional de Estadística, Geografía e Informática [INEGI], 1986), p. 5; United Nations, Comisión Económica para América Latina, *Evolución de la frontera norte, 1940–1986* (Mexico, D.F.: United Nations, 1987), p. 30; Jorge Carrillo, ed., *Mercados de trabajo en la industria maquiladora de exportación* (Mexico: Secretaría del Trabajo y Previsión Social/Colegio de la Frontera Norte, 1991); Norris C. Clement and Stephen Jenner, "La industria maquiladora de México y la economía de California," in *Las maquiladoras: Ajuste estructural y desarrollo regional,* ed. Bernardo González Aréchiga and Rocío Barajas Escamilla (Tijuana: Colegio de la Frontera Norte, Fundación Friedrich Ebert, 1989), p. 125; Universidad Autónoma de Baja California, *Estadísticas sobre la fuerza de trabajo femenina en Mexicali: Participación en la industria de transformación y repercusiones en la familia* (Mexicali: Universidad Autónoma de Baja California, Instituto de Investigaciones Sociales, 1984), pp. 16–35; Norris C. Clement et al., *Maquiladora Resource Guide: Exploring the Maquiladora/In-Bond Option in Baja California, Mexico* (San Diego: Institute for Regional Studies of the Californias, San Diego State University, 1989), p. 17; Ruíz and Tiano, *Women on the U.S.-Mexico Border.*

11. Stoddard, *Maquila;* Mitchell Selligson and Edward J. Williams, *Maquiladoras and Migration: Workers in the Mexico-United States Border Industrialization Program* (Austin: University of Texas Press, 1981); Sklair, *Assembling for Development;* Clement et al., *Maquiladora Resource Guide;* Richard Rothstein, "A Hand for Mexico, a

Slap for Us," *Los Angeles Times,* November 23, 1990; Wilson, *Exports and Local Development.*

12. See George Baker, "Social Costs and Revenues of the Maquiladora Industry," in Lorey, *United States-Mexico Border Statistics since 1900,* p. 465 and passim.

13. *New York Times,* January 12, 1998.

14. Joel Millman, "There's Your Solution," *Forbes* (January 7, 1991): 72, 76.

15. Tamayo and Fernández, *Zonas fronterizas,* pp. 71–72.

16. Chandler Davidson, *Race and Class in Texas Politics* (Princeton: Princeton University Press, 1990), pp. 262–66; Max R. Sherman, ed., *The Future of Texas* (Austin: Texas Monthly Press, 1988), pp. 5–32, 87–110; M. Ray Perryman, *Survive and Conquer—Texas in the '80s* (Dallas: Taylor Publishing, 1990).

17. See Jesus Sanchez, "Boeing to Slash Aircraft Production 35%," *Los Angeles Times,* January 27, 1993.

18. California Department of Finance, *Economic Report of the Governor: 1988* (Sacramento: California Governor's Office, 1988), pp. 32–35; California Department of Finance, *Economic Report of the Governor, 1990* (Sacramento: California Governor's Office, 1990), pp. 1–2, 21–24, 59–60; California Department of Finance, *Economic Report of the Governor, 1991* (Sacramento: California Governor's Office, 1991), pp. 1–2, 13–31, A15; *New Mexico Business: Current Economic Report* (March 1990): 1–2; *Arizona's Economy* (April 1991): 1–4; *Arizona Progress* (1990): 1–2, 4; U.S. Deptartment of Commerce, Bureau of the Census, *Statistical Abstract of the United States, 1989* (Washington, DC: Government Printing Office, 1989), pp. 367, 377–78, 396; U.S. Department of Labor, Bureau of Labor Statistics, *Employment and Earnings* (February 1992): 160–64; U.S. Department of Labor, Bureau of Labor Statistics, *Employment and Earnings* (July 1992): 155–59.

CHAPTER SIX

THE CONSEQUENCES
OF RAPID GROWTH
IN THE BORDER REGION

SOCIAL AND CULTURAL CHANGE
SINCE THE 1940s

AFTER WORLD WAR II, industrialization, rapid population growth, and urbanization reshaped the daily lives of border dwellers. Border natives were joined by millions of new immigrants from other areas of the United States, from Central Mexico, and from many other parts of the world. The experiences of border life became more common in both countries, as the states along the boundary claimed an ever larger share of Mexican and U.S. national populations. In the postwar period a complex social mosaic spanning the international boundary emerged from what had been at the beginning of the century two distinct social avant-gardes. In the 1990s no one could describe Los Angeles—or anywhere else along the border—as Octavio Paz had in his 1957 *Labyrinth of Solitude*: "Mexicanism . . . floats in the air . . . 'floats' because it never mixes or unites with the other world, the North American world."[1] The impact of century-long migratory trends and economic integration resulted in a true Mex-America along the international boundary. The U.S.-Mexican border region is expected to be the most populous region in North America by the beginning of the twenty-first century. The sheer number of people is certain to place the social evolution of the border onto both domestic and bilateral agendas. With its social complexities and challenges, life in the region is a portent of future life in the Americas.

POPULATION AND MIGRATION

During the forty-year period from 1950 to 1990, the population of the Mexican border states multiplied 3.5 times, while that of the U.S. border states multiplied 2.6 times (see Table 6-1). The pattern had reversed since the period before 1940, when the rate of increase on the Mexican side of the border was significantly lower than that on the U.S. side. From 1950 forward the population of the Mexican border states rose considerably faster than that of the U.S. border states. Between 1940 and 1990, annual growth was 3.3 percent in the Mexican region, 2.6 percent in the U.S. region, and 2.7 percent in the area as a whole.[2] The rapid demographic upsurge in the Mexican border states was due to both internal migration and higher rates of natural increase than those across the boundary, where growth was fueled primarily by migration.

TABLE 6-1
BORDER-STATE POPULATION, 1950–1990

State	1950	1960	1970	1980	1990
Baja California	226,965	520,165	870,421	1,177,886	1,660,855
Chihuahua	846,414	1,226,793	1,612,525	2,005,477	2,441,873
Coahuila	720,619	907,734	1,114,956	1,557,265	1,972,340
Nuevo León	740,191	1,078,848	1,694,689	2,513,044	3,098,736
Sonora	510,607	783,378	1,098,720	1,513,731	1,823,606
Tamaulipas	718,167	1,024,182	1,456,858	1,924,484	2,249,581
Mexican Border	3,762,963	5,541,100	7,848,169	10,691,887	13,246,991
Mexican Total	25,791,017	34,923,129	48,225,238	66,846,833	81,249,645
Arizona	749,587	1,302,161	1,775,399	2,718,215	3,665,228
California	10,586,223	15,717,204	19,871,069	23,667,902	29,760,021
New Mexico	681,187	951,023	1,017,055	1,302,894	1,515,069
Texas	7,711,194	9,579,677	11,188,655	14,229,191	16,986,510
U.S. Border	19,728,191	27,550,065	33,852,178	41,918,202	51,926,828
U.S. Total	151,325,798	179,323,175	203,302,031	226,545,805	248,709,873

Source: Lorey, *United States-Mexico Border Statistics since 1900,* Table 100.

As a whole the area along the international boundary came to claim an ever greater share of the total national populations of both countries. The four U.S. border states grew from 6.4 percent of the national total in 1900 to 20.9 percent by 1990. California, which had become the most populous U.S. state by the early 1960s, claimed 57.3 percent of the border population in 1990; one of every nine U.S. citizens lived in California. In Mexico the border states accounted for 10.3 percent of the national population in 1900 and 16.3 percent in 1990. By 1990 the ten border states in the two countries were home to sixty-five million people. Unlike the U.S. region, with its concentration of people in the two states of California and Texas, the Mexican region had a relatively even distribution in its six northernmost states.

The dimensions of the migrant flows to the boundary area—from East to West within the United States, to the North within Mexico, and across the border—expanded dramatically after the early 1940s. Large numbers of new migrants were pushed out of central Mexico by rapid population growth, declining opportunity in the countryside, and insufficient employment in industry in comparison with the number of people entering the job market. Frequently, migrants were drawn by significantly greater opportunity—more jobs and higher wage levels—in both the Mexican and U.S. border states. Building on both personal experiences of migration and the social networks created by migrant populations, the flow of people grew and changed apace with the increasing economic integration of Mexico and the United States.

In the United States, World War II and the jobs it created drew an enormous number of people west. In the brief period of the war years alone, two million migrants headed to California, attracted by high-paying jobs in wartime industries such as steel, shipbuilding, aircraft manufacture, textiles, and services. In the war decade from 1940 to 1950, eight million people moved to states west of the Mississippi River, 44 percent of them to California.

The wartime economic boom in the United States drew Mexican migrants north. Inhabitants of rural areas in Mexico, many of whom had been negatively affected by the rapid commercialization of agriculture after the 1930s, moved first to regional urban centers and then frequently toward the border. Swiftly growing cities on the Mexican side of the international boundary—Tijuana, Hermosillo, and Mexicali, for instance—became staging areas for migrants seeking to relocate to both the Mexican countryside and U.S. urban conglomerations north of the border.[3]

Mexican migration to the border states in the postwar period was not uniform throughout the region; rather, it tended to follow economic developments in the United States. In the late nineteenth and early twentieth centuries, when Texas experienced significant development, the largest cities in the Mexican North had been Ciudad Juárez and Monterrey. During and after World War II, as California overtook Texas in economic development, an enormous migration began in a more westerly direction. In Baja California, the previously small towns of Tijuana and Mexicali became major cities, while Ensenada, Tecate, San Luis Río Colorado, Hermosillo, and Nogales also increased in size. The extraordinary growth of Tijuana and Mexicali led to the achievement of statehood for the province of Baja California Norte, which entered the federal republic as Baja California in 1952. Statehood followed for Baja California Sur in 1974.[4]

The bracero agreements between the United States and Mexico, which arranged for the legal transfer of hundreds of thousands of Mexican temporary workers across the border, facilitated migration to the United States throughout the entire postwar period. Many braceros stayed permanently in the United States and then brought their extended families north. The Bracero Program established an advance guard and also stimulated networks that continue to direct a flow of Mexicans to the United States to this day.

Beyond its direct effects the Bracero Program had important social consequences. The seemingly inexhaustible supply of hard-working Mexican laborers kept wages low in U.S. agriculture and conditioned U.S. employers to the immediate availability of inexpensive field labor. Large agribusinesses were among the major supporters of flexible immigration policy; the pressure they brought to bear helped maintain a steady supply of low-cost Mexican labor throughout the postwar era. The program also encouraged an increased flow of both documented and undocumented migrants to the United States after the 1940s.

The Bracero Program left a definite imprint on border towns. Men brought north to work in the program passed through border towns in a steady stream. Those who stayed on in Mexico's North swelled the population of those cities, frequently moving their families from the interior in order to be close to them during the off season. Further contributing to the floating population of border cities were deportations carried out by the U.S. Immigration and Naturalization Service (INS), which took illegal entrants from central and southern Mexico and dropped them at the border, where they often remained permanently.

The Bracero Program also encouraged the attitude that Mexican workers could be returned to Mexico when they were no longer needed, a belief that had important social ramifications. The infamous Operation Wetback of 1953–1955 deported two million Mexicans (and many U.S. citizens of Mexican heritage) to the region across the boundary. This massive repatriation effort had the effect of transferring to the Mexican border

Immigrant Mexican laborers, Imperial Valley, California.
Paul Ganster, Institute for Regional Studies of the Californias

states the social dislocations caused by the economic slowdown in U.S. agriculture following the Korean War.[5] But even the deportation of two million Mexicans had little effect on the overall trend of rapid population growth and migration in the border states.

Critics of the Bracero Program charged numerous abuses, including the failure by employers to pay wages, the forced deportation of laborers after work had been performed, pesticide and herbicide poisoning, lengthy work days, and unhealthful and unsafe conditions. Formal provisions for wages, hours, transportation, and housing were frequently violated. Migrant farm laborers tended to live in generalized poverty.[6] In fact, both domestic agricultural workers in the U.S. border states and migrants had long suffered from low pay, piecework rates that resulted in excessive hours, unenforced contracts, exposure to pesticides, and unfavorable conditions. Critics affiliated with a wide spectrum of labor, civil rights, church, and social activist organizations argued that the migration of Mexican farmhands depressed wages further, undermined the bargaining power of U.S. workers, and denied employment to U.S. citizens.

Both the promises and the pitfalls of migration during the 1940s and 1950s are borne out by the personal experiences of braceros. Manuel Padilla, interviewed by border historian Oscar Martínez, tells of his constant conflicts with employers over the letter and the spirit of the bracero contract system. Beginning in 1946, Padilla, who originally had registered as a bracero in Aguascalientes and then signed up three additional times in Mexicali, worked for a decade picking and loading lemons, oranges, and apples in California and Washington State. After a time, Padilla deserted his bracero contract, spent many years in the United States as an undocumented laborer, and eventually became a permanent resident in 1956.[7]

Crossing the border was difficult and could be treacherous for those without documents. In a classic story by Ted Conover about these hazards, the migrant Jesús and his comrades are tormented by Mexican migration and customs inspectors, who extort money from them, and by the Mexican state police, who beat up some members of the party and demand bribe money. After paying a series of *coyotes*, who smuggle immigrants into the

United States, Jesús passes through Arizona only to be stopped in Utah and returned to Mexico. After several more days attempting to cross and making additional payoffs, Jesús arrives in Idaho, where he had arranged for a number of years of regular employment on a ranch. After a few months of work, Jesús returns to Mexico for the winter.[8]

In the last thirty or so years of the twentieth century, a sizable share of the internal migration of Mexicans to the country's North, and some part of the migration across the international boundary, was linked to the development of *maquila* assembly plants along the far northern rim of Mexico after 1965. The principal social impact of *maquila* development in the Mexican border states was the provision of steady employment with what were, at least in the Mexican context, high wages and generous nonwage benefits. In the period from 1978 to 1993 *maquila* jobs grew at an annual rate of 14 percent, far outpacing the rate of job creation in Mexico as a whole. In addition, unemployment in the Mexican border states was generally far below central Mexican levels.

Firsthand accounts from the 1980s and 1990s, by which time whole families were frequently caught up in the migrant flow, give testimony to the social and cultural difficulties attendant upon those who lived the transboundary experience, whether in the field or in the factory. For Zacatecan Jesús Avila, age thirty-one; his wife, age twenty-nine; and their three children ages seven to eleven, repeat migration to the United States became a way of life. The family lived in the United States one year and returned to Mexico the next. Even with migration, Avila's earnings barely sustained the family. Avila invested some of his wages in a peach-growing venture in Mexico, but a constant income from migrant employment was needed to sustain the operation. Although he hoped to settle permanently in California, Luis López, age thirty-three, used migrant earnings to make additions on his house in Mexico. Despite evident economic gains from migration, López told an interviewer, "It is very sad to go [to the United States], and in my heart I would not go except for the necessity which obliges one to do such things. . . . My children respect me because they know that they should; but . . . my family has begun to distance itself from me."[9]

URBANIZATION

Although many North Americans think of the U.S. West as made up of wide-open sparsely populated spaces and pastoral occupations, a highly urban profile characterizes the area. The West is, in fact, the most urban region of the United States, perhaps because such concentration was inevitable in the development of a "hydraulic society" in the arid regions of the border states. The border states of the West, already more urban than rural by 1930, grew from 55.1 percent urban in 1930 to 56.9 percent in 1940, 71.5 percent in 1950, 81.2 percent in 1960, 86 percent in 1970, 86.3 percent in 1980, and 87.7 in 1990. The percentage of persons living in urban areas of the United States as a whole was significantly lower in 1990—75.2 percent.

The great postwar migration of Mexican and U.S. citizens to the border states was overwhelmingly to urban areas. Whereas the Bracero Program of the 1940s led Mexican migrants, legal and illegal, primarily to rural areas and agricultural employment, by the 1960s the flow was to large urban concentrations for jobs in manufacturing, construction, hotels, restaurants, and services. In Mexico, peasants fleeing crushing rural poverty could either migrate to Mexico's cities or search for work north of the border. Many of those who headed north got no farther than Mexico's border cities, contributing to accelerated urbanization in that region. It is estimated that in 1974 one-quarter to one-third of the population of Mexico's border cities consisted of recent migrants.[10] In the 1970s, 1980s, and on into the 1990s, Mexicans increasingly pursued opportunities in U.S. border cities—a natural shift, given the changing economies of the border states—especially in the service sector and in industry. New cities sprouted up throughout the U.S. West, while previously small towns such as Phoenix boomed and old cities such as Los Angeles grew into megalopolises. Fully 80 percent of all Mexican migrants to California, for example, settled in urban areas in both the northern and southern parts of the state; 55 percent settled in Los Angeles.[11]

The Mexican North, where small towns and villages had been more common, also experienced the development of urban concentrations. Monterrey, Nuevo León, already a large city by the standards of the Mexican North in 1940, with almost 200,000 inhabitants, grew to more than one million by 1980. Desert cities such as Chihuahua and Hermosillo grew rapidly, as they expanded beyond traditional rural economic pursuits into industry and services. By 1990, 84.7 percent of the population of the Mexican border states lived in urban areas, in contrast with 42.5 percent in 1940. Mirroring a national reality, the rapidly growing urban populations of the Mexican North came to be dominated by recent migrants from rural areas. By the 1980s the nonnative population of Ciudad Juárez was 53 percent and that of Tijuana was 66 percent. The urban areas on the Mexican side of the border were densely populated, with the cores of the municipalities (*municipios*) generally claiming at least 65 percent and sometimes as much as 95 percent of the municipal population.

As with the western United States, urbanization in Mexico's north was a natural consequence of the arid environment, since development depended on vast, capital-intensive, centrally managed waterworks. Additionally, Mexico and much of the U.S. Southwest were influenced by the Hispanic tradition of such centralizing outposts as missions, pueblos, and presidios, which also included the practice of superimposing settlements over preexisting indigenous communities or bringing scattered indigenous villages together into a single regional settlement. Because of this urban emphasis, Mexico's northern tier of states remained relatively unpopulated outside of the cities. In 1990, while Mexico's population density stood at 41.5 inhabitants per square kilometer, the six border states had an average density of only 16.7.[12] Reflecting the concentration of the northern population in a few major urban areas, Monterrey's share of Nuevo León's population climbed from 40 percent in 1940 to 77 percent in 1980.

By midcentury a pattern of twin cities had emerged all along the international boundary from Tijuana-San Diego on the Pacific to Matamoros-Brownsville on the Gulf Coast (see Table 6-2). Each twin-city pair shared some characteristics of expansion and differed in others. San Diego grew with World War II and the expansion of area military bases, while Tijuana grew apace as a tourist center for both military personnel and southern Californians interested in the gambling and the nightlife. Ciudad Juárez and El Paso expanded together as an important commercial hub straddling the

TABLE 6-2
TWIN-CITY POPULATIONS, 1900–1990

Twin Cities	1900	1910	1920	1930	1940	1950	1960	1970	1980	1990
Matamoros, Tamaulipas	8,347	7,390	9,215	9,733	15,699	45,846	92,627	137,749	188,703	266,055
Brownsville, Texas	6,305	10,517	11,791	22,021	22,083	36,066	48,040	52,522	84,997	98,962
Reynosa, Tamaulipas	1,915	1,475	2,107	4,840	9,412	34,087	74,140	137,383	194,657	265,663
McAllen, Texas	—	—	5,331	9,074	11,877	20,067	32,728	37,636	66,281	89,021
Nuevo Laredo, Tamaulipas	6,548	8,143	14,998	21,636	28,872	57,668	92,327	148,867	201,690	218,413
Laredo, Texas	13,492	14,855	22,710	32,618	39,274	51,510	60,678	69,024	91,449	122,899
Piedras Negras, Coahuila	7,888	8,518	6,941	15,878	15,663	27,581	44,992	41,033	67,444	96,178
Eagle Pass, Texas	—	3,536	5,765	5,059	6,459	7,267	12,094	15,364	21,407	20,651
Ciudad Juárez, Chihuahua	8,218	10,621	19,457	19,669	48,881	112,467	262,119	407,370	544,496	789,522
El Paso, Texas	15,906	39,279	77,560	102,421	96,810	130,485	276,687	322,261	425,259	515,342
Nogales, Sonora	2,738	3,117	13,445	14,061	13,866	24,478	37,657	52,108	65,587	105,873
Nogales, Arizona	—	3,514	5,199	6,006	5,135	6,153	7,286	8,946	15,683	19,489
Mexicali, Baja California	—	462	6,782	14,842	18,775	64,609	174,540	263,498	341,559	438,377
Calexico, California	—	797	6,223	6,299	5,415	6,433	7,992	10,625	14,412	18,633
Tijuana, Baja California	242	733	1,028	8,384	16,486	59,952	152,374	277,306	429,500	698,752
San Diego, California	17,700	39,978	74,683	147,897	203,341	334,387	573,224	697,027	875,538	1,110,549

Source: Lorey, *United States-Mexico Border Statistics since 1900,* Table 110.

lines of communication from northern Mexico to the U.S. Midwest. This development would facilitate the transformation of Ciudad Juárez into the most important center of the *maquiladora* industry in the 1970s, 1980s, and 1990s.[13] Over time, growth shifted from a larger urban center in the U.S. twin city to a larger urban center on the Mexican side of the border.

The twin-city pairs developed complex interrelationships and interdependencies. Table 6-3 shows the massive flow of people back and forth across the border between Tijuana and San Diego. By 1990 two-way traffic crossing the border, most of it commuters, tourists, and shoppers, exceeded 274 million per year—a number greater than the population of the United States and three times that of Mexico.[14] Mexican laborers, particularly those employed in services, traveled daily from one twin city to the other to work in U.S. hotels, restaurants, and private homes. An estimated 10 percent of the San Diego civilian work force in 1976 consisted of undocumented Mexican nationals, many of whom came from permanent homes south of the border to work.[15]

Twin cities were populated by a fascinating array of people. In his *Border People*, Martínez has developed a schema for understanding the social landscape of the border's urban world. He includes in his typology of

TABLE 6-3
ENTRY OF MEXICANS AND U.S. CITIZENS AT U.S. BORDER (TIJUANA TO SAN DIEGO),
1928–1990 (IN MILLIONS)

Years	Total	Mexicans	U.S. Citizens
1928–1930	81	49	32
1931–1940	224	137	87
1941–1950	360	195	165
1950	48	24	24
1955	71	36	35
1960	98	59	39
1965	116	69	47
1970	145	87	58
1975	159	98	61
1980	163	104	59
1985	177	108	69
1990	274	173	101

Source: Lorey, *United States-Mexico Border Statistics since 1900*, Table 900.

This neighborhood in Tijuana has no paved streets, water, or electricity.
Paul Ganster, Institute for Regional Studies of the Californias

border social experience the following groups: transient migrants (Mexicans or U.S. citizens residing only briefly in the border region); newcomers (Mexicans or U.S. citizens newly arrived in the region); nationalists (long-term residents of the border who do not participate in the culture of the other side of the boundary, strongly preferring customs that they identify as either Mexican or American); uniculturalists (people who live wholly in the culture of one side); binational consumers (persons whose main experience with the other side of the border is commercial); settler migrants; commuters who move back and forth across the border on a regular (frequently daily) basis to work; biculturalists (persons, generally bilingual, who have roots in and live adult lives on both sides of the border); binationalists (people, frequently businesspeople and professionals who live and do business on both sides of the border, operating at a very high level of transboundary social integration); winter residents (U.S. citizens who spend winter months in the region); and U.S. citizens who reside permanently (frequently after retirement) in the Mexican border states. In addition, Martínez describes some cities along the U.S. border—Laredo, for example—in which the Mexican-origin population has dominated politics and business and the European-origin population has sometimes felt marginal or marginalized.[16]

In the twin-city complexes Mexican consumers on both sides of the border became an important market for North American businesses. Many U.S. firms attributed one-half of their income to Mexican customers traveling from the twin city across the border. It has been estimated that in 1995, cash-carrying Mexican crossers may have spent as much as 5 billion dollars in El Paso's shopping areas (including the huge Cielo Vista and Basset Center malls). An estimated 412 million dollars in U.S. taxes were paid on those purchases.[17] At the same time, a reverse flow brought U.S. citizens daily into Mexico. Between 1973 and 1977 the more than fourteen million U.S. citizens who traveled annually to Tijuana provided a major infusion into its economy. U.S. citizens crossed the border to shop, eat, and take advantage of low prices for such services as dental hygiene, automotive repair, and medical consultations.

Much disparity existed between border cities sharing these important interconnections. A view from the air at any point over the international boundary revealed a sprawling, hastily built, partly unpaved Mexican city with a significant number of temporary shanties inhabited by the most recent and poorest migrants. Rapid growth, combined with the lack of a robust tax base, outpaced the ability of border communities to provide urban services, housing, and social programs to incorporate new migrants. The U.S. side showed a smaller urban settlement with modern public services and transportation facilities. Within this general pattern of asymmetry were significant differences in wages and rates of un- and underemployment in the border cities of the United States and Mexico.[18]

With rapid population growth in the U.S. cities along the international boundary came serious social problems that would soon characterize the West and the border region as a whole: traffic congestion, environmental degradation, a rise in crime, increases in divorce rates, ethnic strife (in an area of great and growing ethnic diversity), and the rapid spread of diseases, including HIV. All of these problems and more stemmed from the frenetic pace of development along the border and from human interactions in its urban oases—from both economic booms and massive population movements. Informal settlements—generally called *colonias*—sprang up all along the U.S. side of the border. For the most part illegal, they lacked even the most basic human services, as evidenced by county health and other social indicators ranking the settlements at the bottom of the nation.

The meteoric growth of Mexican border cities after 1950 resulted in pressing social problems. The most severe concerned underdeveloped public-service infrastructure. From early in the postwar period the rapid increase in population outpaced the development of social services in the region. In 1942, 4,500 students were left without classrooms. This number tripled by the early 1950s. With respect to housing, *El Continental* reported on the conditions of 12,000 persons in Ciudad Juárez in 1948, saying, "[They live] in a very critical situation . . . , suffering horrible needs. In July of 1953, three quarters of the population of Juárez was without drinking water and sewage services: 400 poor children died in a three-month period. They lack the most indispensable services, such as water, sewage, light, police service, telephone, transportation, etc."[19] *El Fronterizo* reported, "Thousands live under incredible conditions, in shacks . . .

built on public lands . . . having no public services. The residents lack sufficient elements to maintain their health and are in need of adequate food. In those areas where conditions are the worst, an alarming rate of infant mortality has been recorded."[20] The public-services crisis on the border is clearly not a new phenomenon; rather, it emerged in the immediate postwar era as a function of the border's pattern of urban growth.

The lack of basic services for a major portion of the urban population along the Mexican border created an enormous public-health problem, and waterborne diseases became a leading cause of death, particularly among infants. Table 6-4 shows the striking differences between the principal causes of death on the U.S. and Mexican sides of the border: intestinal infections, respiratory diseases, and nutritional deficiencies, which topped the list in Mexico, did not appear at all in the U.S. list.[21] In addition, the rate of death from all causes was much higher on the Mexican side than on the U.S. side. As a consequence of these and other factors, there was a five-year difference between the average life expectancy in the Mexican and the U.S. border states in 1980–1984 (life expectancy was 69.4 years in Mexico and 74.4 in the United States).[22]

On the Mexican side of the border, poverty appeared to have increased during the 1970s and 1980s. Minimum-wage data suggest that, after the mid-1970s, real wages for unskilled work declined precipitously in the border region. From 1981 to 1986—during the darkest moments of the 1980s economic crisis in Mexico—the real purchasing power of the minimum wage on the Mexican side of the border dropped by half, diminishing to precarious levels in comparison with the income of Mexico's northern neighbors. By the mid-1980s, Mexicans had fewer dollars to spend in San Diego, yet they felt greater pressure to find work both there and in neighboring Los Angeles.[23] Because of the proximity of the Mexican North to the United States, the cost of living was significantly higher than in other areas of Mexico.

Most Mexican immigrants to the border region lived in homemade houses for years before electricity, potable water, or sewage lines reached their neighborhoods. In Tijuana the average number of inhabitants in individual housing units increased by one-third between 1960 and the

TABLE 6-4
LEADING CAUSES OF DEATH AMONG BORDER CHILDREN AGED 1 TO 4
IN THE LATE 1980s (INCIDENT PER HUNDRED THOUSAND INHABITANTS)

Cause of Death	Mexico (Nationwide)	Baja California	Chihuahua	Coahuila	Nuevo León	Sonora	Tamaulipas
Intestinal infections	107.1	15.3	5.5	16.1	13.9	10.7	18.0
Diseases of the respiratory system	55.0	14.7	10.3	18.4	12.3	14.6	13.8
Nutritional deficiencies	19.1	2.9	1.8	2.3	3.7	4.3	4.6
Congenital anomalies	13.0	4.7	4.1	8.3	12.9	5.6	8.8
Diseases of the nervous system	12.1	6.5	4.4	5.5	5.5	6.5	9.2
All causes	**356.7**	**119.6**	**76.7**	**91.2**	**88.5**	**101.5**	**98.4**

Cause of Death	U.S. (Nationwide)	Arizona	California	New Mexico	Texas
Accidents	19.6	—	—	25.7	23.1
Congenital anomalies	6.3	—	—	8.2	4.8
Malignant tumors	3.7	—	3.4	1.8	2.6
Homicide	2.6	—	2.1	4.6	2.7
Heart diseases	2.4	—	1.4	0.9	2.9
All causes	**50.9**	**63.2**	**48.9**	**58.7**	**52.7**

Source: PAHO, *U.S.-Mexico Border Health Statistics*, 6th ed. (El Paso, TX: PAHO, December 1990).

mid-1980s.[24] Natural disasters such as the winter storms and floods of 1992–93 made the weaknesses of both housing and health-care infra-structure painfully obvious.[25] Although the situation gradually improved after 1950, in 1990 an average 80 percent of houses in border areas were equipped with piped water and only 57 percent with sewerage. In the late 1980s in Tijuana these social conditions and the lack of public services to address them gave rise to a broad political mobilization by the city's pop-ular sectors to gain the attention of regional and national leaders.[26]

As Mexico's border cities matured socially and economically, and their social problems grew, they began to play a greater role in regional and national politics. Although Mexican politics had long been characterized by centralization and control from Mexico City, the North had traditionally been among the more recalcitrant regions. The 1810 independence move-ment began in what had been the North of that period, and the leaders of the 1910 Revolution included such northerners as Madero, Carranza, Obregón, and Calles. Admittedly, during the postrevolutionary period the northern states generally remained firmly under the control of the ruling party, the Partido Revolucionario Institucional (PRI). But by the 1980s sig-nificant opposition challenged the PRI's hegemony.

Political resistance to the central government and increasing demands for tax receipts and other aid—stimulated in part by the country's economic crisis and in part by the North's social and economic maturation—expressed itself dramatically at the polls beginning in the 1980s. The conservative Par-tido de Acción Nacional (PAN) claimed several election victories, partic-ularly in Chihuahua, where it won the sharply contested mayor's office in Ciudad Juárez in 1983. In 1989 the first non-PRI candidate ever to win a gubernatorial election in Mexico, PAN's Ernesto Ruffo, former mayor of Ensenada, became the governor of Baja California. In 1992 another PAN candidate, Francisco Barrio, took the statehouse in Chihuahua. These victories in the North were soon joined by PAN victories on the national level, in central states, and in the congress. In 1997, PAN governed six of Mexico's thirty-one states and the second- and third-largest urban areas—Guadalajara and Monterrey. In 1998, PRI recaptured the Chihuahua gov-ernorship, resulting in the first democratic alternation in Mexico's postrevolutionary history. A social consolidation based on geographical distance from Mexico City and increasing interdependence with the United States thus created a distinct political culture in the Mexican North. By the closing years of the twentieth century, the North's politics and politicians were again shaping the nation's evolution.

MEXICAN AMERICANS

The Mexican-origin population in the U.S. border states grew steadily throughout the twentieth century, as a tide of Mexicans was drawn by the economic expansion of the U.S. West and the progressive integration of the two national economies. Gradually, they moved north through Mexico, crossed the border, and spread throughout the U.S. Southwest, eventually settling as far as Colorado, Washington State, and Chicago. Between 1900 and 1990 the Mexican-origin population in California grew more than 750 times, in Texas it increased more than 153 times, and in the United States as a whole it grew about 131 times (see Table 6-5).[27]

By the second half of the century—as a consequence of both natural increase and continued population movements from Mexico to the United States that resulted in naturalization and permanent residence—the Mexican-born and Mexican-origin population of the U.S. border states

TABLE 6-5
U.S. POPULATION OF MEXICAN ORIGIN, BY STATE, 1900–1990

Year	Arizona	California	New Mexico	Texas
1900	14,172	8,086	6,649	71,062
1910	29,987	33,694	11,918	125,016
1920	61,580	88,771	20,272	251,827
1930	47,855	191,346	15,983	262,672
1940	24,902	134,312	8,875	159,266
1950	24,917	162,309	9,666	196,077
1960	105,342	695,643	34,459	655,523
1970	239,811	1,857,267	119,049	1,619,064
1980	396,410	3,637,466	233,772	2,752,487
1990	616,195	6,070,637	328,836	10,906,488

Source: Lorey, *United States-Mexico Border Statistics since 1900*, Tables 120 and 122.

was already large and was still growing rapidly. Sixty percent of all U.S. Hispanics were found in the four border states and Colorado, according to the census of 1980. The urban centers of the late twentieth-century West were characterized by their Mexican-American population concentrations: in the early 1980s 14.9 percent of residents identified themselves as Latino in San Diego, 27.5 percent in Los Angeles, 62.5 percent in El Paso, 87.3 percent in Brownsville, and 93 percent in Laredo.[28] Although the Mexican-origin population of the border region is the focus here, it is noteworthy that the U.S. border states were characterized in general by the highest rates of foreign-born and foreign-origin population in the country.

By 1990 the border's Mexican-origin population was 16.8 percent of the total population in Arizona, 20.6 percent in California, 21.7 percent in New Mexico, and 22.9 percent in Texas. One of the most noticeable impacts of these large numbers was on the language of the border region: in 1990, 14.2 percent of Arizonans, 20 percent of Californians, 22.1 percent of Texans, and 27.9 percent of New Mexicans spoke Spanish at home.[29]

In *Border People,* Martínez includes the following groups in his typology of Mexican Americans: disadvantaged immigrants (upwardly mobile persons from poorer Mexican-origin U.S. families), advantaged immigrants (U.S. citizens originating in advantaged sectors of Mexican society), binational consumers, commuters who cross the border on a regular basis to work, biculturalists, binationalists, and U.S.-born Mexican Americans who live and work on the Mexican side of the border.[30]

For the substantial minority of Mexican Americans employed in agriculture and living in the countryside in the U.S. border states, life was difficult; insecurity—both physical and financial—was ever present. The plight of Mexican and Mexican-American farmworkers, both legal and illegal residents of the United States, led to increasing political organization and militancy. The 1966 victories of César Chávez against grape growers in California led to the growing solidarity of Mexican and Mexican-American farmworkers throughout California and other border states. That same year, partially in response to issues in border agriculture, the U.S. Congress extended federal minimum-wage laws to agricultural work. Migrant

Mexican-American field laborers, who were often segregated residentially, confronted a frequently hostile environment by creating mutual aid societies, churches, and organizations to promote patriotic and social activities. They and their families reinforced a sense of identity and community by establishing Spanish-language newspapers, some of which exist to this day. Distinct cultural forms came to characterize life for Mexican migrants north of the border. New challenges presented themselves in the 1980s and 1990s, and old problems resurfaced, as non-Spanish-speaking migrants from deep in Mexico's interior—particularly from Oaxaca state—moved to the fields of the Californias.

The poverty of Mexican farmworkers was frequently matched by that of urban-dwelling Mexican Americans. Data show that poverty was widespread among Mexican-American families and that, among all ethnic groups, Mexican Americans were generally the poorest.[31] The occupational structure of El Paso, Texas, in the period from 1910 to 1970 sheds light on the long-term evolution of the employment profile of the Mexican-American population in the United States. While the number of persons with Spanish surnames employed in unskilled and domestic occupations declined from 57.4 percent in 1910 to 23.5 percent in 1970, the number of those employed in skilled positions decreased as well, from 12.8 percent to 7.4 percent. Those workers did not move far, however: employment in semiskilled and service occupations rose from 17 percent to 33.7 percent over the same period. Movement into the uppermost strata was slow but steady, from 11.2 percent to 29.2 percent in lower white-collar occupations and from 1.6 to 6.3 in upper white-collar positions between 1910 and 1970.[32]

Not all urban families of Mexican origin were poor; some had experienced significant social mobility from one generation to another. Although the prevailing popular conception was of poor and downtrodden immigrant families, several studies in the 1990s revealed a large and stable Mexican-American middle class in such border cities as Los Angeles. In the mid-1990s, middle-class Latino families purchased more than one-half of the houses in Los Angeles County and owned one-quarter of all businesses in the Los Angeles-Long Beach metro area (up from 10 percent in the 1980s). Fifty percent of U.S.-born Latino families had household incomes above the national average. The wealth of second-generation migrant families was increasingly reflected in political clout. In the 1996 California state elections, Latinos won fourteen of eighty seats as well as the top leadership posts in the lower house of the legislature.[33]

THE IMPACT OF MIGRATION
ON SENDING COMMUNITIES

Debates over migration in the postwar period tended to focus on its putative effects on the economy and society of the U.S. border states. Observers only infrequently pondered the impacts south of the international boundary. Was migration (and reliance on migrant earnings) a benefit or a detriment *to areas of origin*? What was the impact of migration to the United States on families and communities *in the Mexican border states*? These questions are crucial to an understanding of the larger border world. Because migration and migrant remittances are structural features of local economies throughout Mexico and the United States, both national economies are greatly affected by migrant flows. In many sending communities 41 percent of all household heads had made at least one trip to work in the United States; 81 percent of household heads had a friend or relative living in the United States.[34]

One recent study of Zacatecas and Coahuila shows that well over one-half of all families in both states participated in migration to the United States at some point. Communities with the most diversified local economies tended to have the highest rate of migration. Migrants tended to be male and were younger and more educated than nonmigrants. Within these general parameters there were many regional differences. In Zacatecas, migrants generally came from rural backgrounds and were married with young children. In Coahuila, migrants were more likely to be from urban backgrounds and were less compelled by economic necessity.

Migrant families earned more and owned more than families without this link to the United States. Migrant wages, instead of being wasted in conspicuous consumption, were generally invested in human capital—such as education and medical care—and in sustaining and improving rural livelihoods through the purchase of tractors, land, insecticides, fertilizers, seed, and the like. Income was also dedicated to such family businesses as markets, restaurants, pharmacies, and studios. Commercial knowledge gained through migration frequently proved as important as savings in these cases.

Analysts found some troubling effects of migration on the sending communities. Clearly, migration benefited families and individuals, for example, but earnings were not generally used to support community projects such as recreation centers or churches. Although migrant earnings reduced the gap between rural and urban incomes, they tended to increase the disparity among families within communities. And as its importance as a strategy of human-capital investment registered, migration sometimes discouraged the pursuit of education in Mexican sending communities. Not everyone viewed such effects as bad, however. The replacement of a narrow social elite with a broad-based migrant economic group, breaking the subservience of the peasant classes in rural Mexico, seemed to some observers as a trend that boded well for Mexico. Migration could serve as an alternative mobility ladder.[35]

Remittances from migrants to their families in Mexico made both indirect and direct positive contributions to the sending communities. Through increased consumption and investment, savings were transmitted to other households in migrant-sending areas, including some that did not participate directly in international migration. By providing access to liquid savings, such earnings influenced the use of other income, loosening credit constraints on investment and local production. Migrants promoted investment by offering informal insurance against loss, promising to assist in times of economic distress or in the event that new investments failed.[36] These economic bonds between migrants and sending communities created entire transboundary social worlds. Encarnación Allende, age thirty-nine and a U.S. citizen, is a good example. In the 1980s, Allende worked as a groundskeeper at a San Antonio golf course, commuting back to Mexico every few weeks to be with his wife and three children in Coahuila, where he invested much of his earnings. Allende's transboundary life, made possible by remittances and investment of income, was a result of his wife's feelings of estrangement and rejection in the United States, which had led to her insistence on living in Mexico.[37]

Migration is thus woven into the fabric of societies on both sides of the border, "linking villages in Mexico and the U.S. economy so pervasively that the two form a single economic space that transcends the . . . border." Through migration, communities in Mexico and communities in the United States became part of a transboundary organism, a web of relationships bounded by the northward flow of migrants and by the southward flow of remittances.[38] The following figures give some idea of the scope of the migration web: In 1994, Latin American remittances were estimated at 5.5 billion dollars, 3.7 billion dollars of which came from Mexican migrants to family members in Mexico.[39] This meant that—along with petroleum, manufactured exports, and tourism—migrant earnings sent to Mexico constituted one of the country's top sources of foreign exchange.

CULTURAL EVOLUTIONS

Reflecting the economic and social consolidation described here and in previous chapters, the culture of the U.S.-Mexican border region grew increasingly rich and varied in the twentieth century, particularly after World War II. Cultural expression was shaped by three factors: geographical mobility (primarily the circular and one-way migrant flows between the United States and Mexico), the characteristic livelihoods of the area, and the growing social and political awareness of the people. In contrast to earlier periods the border itself—as both a barrier and a unifier—came to figure prominently in regional cultural expression. Cultural manifestations in the border states were characterized by a sense of both pride and ambiguity about the area encompassed in the elusive and shifting boundary. In ethnic terms, border culture reflected a social milieu that was both a melting pot and a salad bowl. There were mixed feelings about Mexico, the United States, Mexicans, Americans, Mexican-Americans, *fronterizos*, Americanization, Mexicanization, and, in general, the multicultural, multiethnic society that was an inescapable facet of daily experience in the region.[40]

Culturally, "the border" implies much more than just the international boundary and the immediate adjacent national territory. The cultural border between the United States and Mexico extends northward beyond San Ysidro or Brownsville, at the very least, as far west as San Francisco and as far east as San Antonio and Houston. There are, additionally, significant pockets of border life and culture in nonborder states, most noticeably in Colorado, in Washington, and in Illinois, in the metropolitan area surrounding Chicago. From the 1940s the cultural border area expanded with agriculture into California's central and coastal valleys, southwest to the agricultural areas of Baja California and Sonora, and southeast to Chihuahua, Coahuila, Tamaulipas, and Texas. Border culture also responded to the shifts in regional industrialization, most recently to the shift of *maquiladora* assembly and manufacturing plants to the interior of Mexico. Southward, border culture meandered from the Mexican Far North down highways to the Central Plateau. Even the Yucatán peninsula, traditionally a world apart but now caught up in the second wave of *maquiladora* expansion, came to exhibit distinctive border-culture traits. It can be argued that the boundary extends into the Gulf of Mexico, which separates the Yucatán from the U.S. South and Florida as an extension of the Rio Grande.

Complicating—and enriching—this picture of an extensive border culture is the fact that it is not monolithic; it takes myriad forms. As Martínez has shown, different groups participate in different aspects of border life and social interaction and consequently display a great variety of cultural traits. "Border society reflect[s] an ongoing process of conflict, exchange, adaptation, and reinvention propelled by class, the character of economic exchange, the area's relation to the national economy, gender, and immigration."[41] The forms of cultural expression are as diverse as the region's population, ranging from habits of dress and social style, to celebrations of community solidarity, to milestones in popular music, film, poetry, and painting. They all share a complex and fruitful interchange among popular tradition and expression, the forms and conventions of high art, and the influence of the national cultures of Mexico and the United States.

As the twentieth century approached, railroad transportation made it increasingly easy for U.S. citizens to travel through Mexico and for Mexicans to travel north. Thousands of U.S. citizens visited or settled in Mexico beginning in the 1880s. On the eve of the fall of the Díaz government, approximately 60,000 Americans lived in Mexico, while the railroads brought multitudes of Mexicans north. A historian of Sonora notes that the railroad itself produced increased social interaction: interpersonal contact, music, sports, and vacationing all increased along its tracks. The railroad created whole new towns and border communities throughout the region, in many places defining for the first time the boundary, which had previously not existed in a social or cultural sense. Sonoran elites began to vacation in Santa Monica; the middle classes traveled to Tucson. The United States became associated with progress, which influenced the selection of names for stores and services throughout the Mexican border states.[42]

Although it is common to see the increasing intensity of interaction among U.S. citizens and Mexicans as an aspect of U.S.-Mexican relations, growing economic integration had its most profound effects locally, on communities on both sides of the border. Because of the presence of U.S. citizens in the Mexican North, Mexicans became familiar with the ways of the *norteamericanos* (North Americans). At the same time, Mexican words, foods, and agricultural and pastoral practices entered U.S. lexicons, lifestyles, and toolboxes. English became the language of business in the border region from the 1880s; it became necessary to learn English to obtain the best jobs in mining, commerce, and commercial agriculture. Globalization of the economy by the 1990s only reinforced the already dominant position of English as the language of trade in Mexico.

Material influences were important in shaping border culture as well. With the arrival of the railroad, U.S. goods altered patterns of consumption throughout the Mexican North. Fashions and foods replaced and shaped local habits, in particular supplanting European varieties, which became much more expensive than their U.S. counterparts.[43] The bicycle craze sweeping Europe and the United States also arrived in the border states, and cycling clubs abounded by the turn of the century. Elites may have held on to French styles and language, but they increasingly sent their children

Magazines provide U.S. border communities with ample
cultural links to the land of origin.
David E. Lorey

to school in the United States. Migrants and merchants introduced the
phonograph, which greatly expanded the repertoire of musical styles, and
the motion-picture projector, which offered a window to life-styles and hap-
penings around the world.

In Sonora commemorative events reflected this early confluence of
cultural currents. Residents of towns and villages all over the state celebrated Independence Day (September 16) and Cinco de Mayo with speeches
and parades. But they also increasingly observed Thanksgiving (after 1901)
and Christmas, both introduced from north of the border. By the turn of
the century, baseball was played in towns and villages throughout the
region. As practices were widely adopted throughout the area, Mexicans
became no more anglicized or Americanized than U.S. citizens became
Mexicanized; rather, an expanded cultural repertoire allowed border residents
to fashion new cultural worlds and to function in the worlds of others.[44]

A store front illustrates the influence of the Spanish language
in border-community businesses.
David E. Lorey

Over time economic and social asymmetries developed along the
international boundary and, with them, more cultural differences and distinction than had existed previously. The towns on the U.S. side of the border experienced a more profound and sustained economic expansion, for
reasons noted in earlier chapters. Inequalities and inequities followed
and were reflected in popular and elite cultural expression. Differences were
particularly noticeable in architecture and public services—from schools
and other public buildings to the houses and recreation areas of inhabitants. Conflicts between—or within—communities straddling the border
became endemic and remain so. Conflicts ranged from small-time violence
to the occasional international incident. Only in very recent times has a
culture of cooperation and exchange gradually emerged in local transboundary conflict resolution, although it faces an entrenched legacy of mis-
trust and misapprehension.

Popular music forms are among the most deeply rooted traditions along the boundary. The border ballad, with its characteristic focus on regional ethnic and cultural conflict, emerged during the Mexican-American War of 1846–1848. The border *corrido* form dates to the same period. In Sonora, formal musical groups originated with local civilian militias in the last third of the nineteenth century. Popular sectors and wealthier residents of border communities had their own musical groups, styles, and events, but there was plenty of crossover. European introductions like the waltz, mazurka, and polka were adapted by local bands and eventually formed the basis of Mexico's classic *norteño* (northern) style.[45]

In their traditional forms the ballad and *corrido* lasted through the Revolution, celebrating revolutionary actors and events, and into the depression era. After World War II the *corrido* underwent a major change in its subject matter, which reflected the evolving social milieu of the border states: the Mexican avenger transformed into a helpless victim. In the 1960s and 1970s the Chicano movement adopted the *corrido* as a strong mobilizing force, replacing the traditional *corrido* hero—frustrated and powerless— with a hero who actively resisted.[46] In the 1990s the *corrido* took up the theme of drug trafficking and its social impacts. After World War II two types of musical groups characteristic of the border continued in popularity: the *conjunto* (ensemble), anchored by the European accordion, and the larger *orquesta* (orchestra).

In the 1980s popular music of the border elbowed its way into the national cultural arena, as Los Angeles-based musicians such as Linda Rondstadt and Los Lobos—following in the footsteps of many lesser-known innovators before them—found national audiences for musical explorations of their Mexican, Mexican-American, and border-region roots.[47] The 1995 death of Texas pop phenomenon Selena was mourned by millions of fans on both sides of the border.

Mural painting, like music a staple of the Mexican popular artistic tradition, found dramatic expression in the border states during the postwar period. The early activism of the Chicano movement inspired many community mural projects, the most famous of which were those in San Diego. Painted during the 1960s and 1970s, freeway-overpass murals in Barrio Logan and wall murals in Balboa Park combined the message of the radical Chicano experience with traditional themes of Mexican popular art. In the Barrio Logan paintings, the cult-icon Mexican painter Frida Kahlo and the Virgin of Guadalupe are found within a few yards of each other, while reinterpretations of border history are juxtaposed with scenes of daily life in Mexico.[48]

Film, which like music and visual expressions provides rich insights into cultural perceptions on both sides of the U.S.-Mexican border, reached a mass audience in the postwar period with its combination of popular and high-art expressions. Postwar U.S. filmic treatments of the border had an auspicious beginning with the 1949 Metro Goldwyn Mayer production, *Border Incident*. The movie was an important landmark for several reasons: the director was the well-respected Arthur Mann; the film was generally devoid of the negative stereotyping typical of the Hollywood cinema of the previous decades; the plot revealed at least some knowledge of and sensibility toward Mexican immigrants in the United States; and Mexican-origin actors were cast in feature roles.[49]

Mexican films on the border had an equally propitious beginning. The first major commercial production was Alejandro Galindos's *Espaldas mojadas*, which premiered in 1954. It was among the most accurate Mexican portrayals of border themes because of its dispassionate look at the socioeconomic problems of Mexico, the hopelessness experienced by countless Mexicans, the need for many to immigrate to the United States, and the conditions in the Mexican-American barrios on the U.S. side of the border.

In terms of quantity, Mexico dominated the production of border films in the postwar period with over two hundred motion pictures. Among the best known are *Siete en la mira*, *Ni de aquí, ni de allá*, *Wetbacks/Mojados*, *Chicano*, *Soy chicano y mexicano*, *Raíces de sangre*, *Mojado Power*, *Murieron a la mitad del río*, *Camelia la Tejana*, and *La Mafia de la frontera*. North American studios also mounted large-scale productions, which were starred in by some of Hollywood's biggest names—Jack Nicholson, Nick Nolte, Tom Cruise, Charles Bronson, María Conchita Alonso, and Shelley Long. Major films included *The Border*, *Borderline*, *Extreme Prejudice*, *Losing It*, *Viva Max*, *Born in East L.A.*, and *The Three Amigos*.

Mexican and U.S. movies about the border shared some similarities. They were almost all filmed for the same basic purpose, commercial success, a goal that influenced their treatment of border themes. Action took precedence over character study, plot development, and social content. Motion pictures dealing with immigration and crime were characterized by violence and sex. The plots were almost always set in the United States and tended to disregard Mexican issues. In the case of comedies, much humor was based on negative stereotypes of Mexicans, U.S. citizens, and border residents.

In both Mexico and the United States, filmmakers working outside the major studios have produced some of the most accurate and moving portrayals of border life. These movies concentrated on the lives, experiences, and perceptions of border residents to create documentaries and works of art that reflect a deep sensitivity toward the complexity of border reality. *El Norte, Alambrista, Break of Dawn*, and *The Ballad of Gregorio Cortez* stand out among these productions.[50]

Literature of the border region blossomed in the period since 1945, especially as the oral traditions, always typical of the area, were incorporated into more formal literary expressions. On the U.S. side, Chicano literature predominated, encompassing border life both thematically and spiritually. Many contemporary Mexican-American writers—José Villarreal, Miguel Mendez, Alurista, Alejandro Morales, Arturo Islas, Margarita Cota Cárdenas, Ernesto Galarza, and Irene Beltrán Hernández—used the border as a setting and inspiration.[51] Equally impressive in quantity and quality was literary expression originating on the Mexican side of the border. An outpouring of anthologies, short-story collections, poetry, plays, and essays made border literature one of the most dynamic and promising of Mexico's regional literatures.[52] In recent years, the border region also witnessed the development of unique currents in critical and feminist theory focusing on the particular problems of the interpretation of works of art produced in the multiethnic, multicultural border states.[53]

In the 1960s the Mexican government attempted to make the border more culturally palatable to both Mexican and prospective U.S. tourists. The PRONAF program discussed in Chapter 5 sought to rehabilitate the reputation of the border region and raise awareness of its cultural riches. Regional museums and cultural centers displayed native arts and crafts. Millions of pesos were invested in commercial and cultural facilities designed to improve the appearance of border cities and promote the sale of Mexican products. In Ciudad Juárez, officials built an attractive new entrance to the city, including a statue of Abraham Lincoln, a large shopping-center complex, hotels, restaurants, an arts-and-crafts center, a Museum of Art and History, a convention building, a country club, a racetrack, and a *charro* (rodeo) ring. The U.S. recession of the early 1970s, among other factors, discouraged travel, however, and the program was only partially successful in drawing new tourists to the border.

The social profile of the postwar border area—which resulted primarily from a century of population movement from east to west and south to north—was clearly as complex as its economy. The social problems confronting the region have been many and diverse, including the health threats of environmental degradation, a spreading public-service crisis, and the widespread psychological and social stresses inherent in the border's multi-ethnic society. The cultural changes that accompanied the emergence of this new society left a unique imprint on the region. With all of these issues, life on the border has presented a unique challenge for scholars and policymakers who attempt to understand and guide the rapidly changing region.

NOTES

1. Octavio Paz, *Labyrinth of Solitude* (New York: Grove Press, 1961), p. 13.
2. Implicit compound rates.
3. For an excellent review of the enormous literature on the causes and consequences of Mexican migration, see Durand and Massey, "Mexican Migration to the United States."
4. Ricardo Romero Aceves, *Baja California: Histórica y legendaria* (Mexico, D.F.: Costa-Amic, 1983), p. 100; Héctor Lucero Antuna, *Evolución política constitucional de Baja California Sur* (Mexico, D.F.: Universidad Nacional Autónoma de Mexico, Instituto de Investigaciones Jurídicas, 1979), p. 24.
5. Juan Ramón García, *Operation Wetback: The Mass Deportation of Mexican Undocumented Workers in 1954* (Westport, CT: Greenwood Press, 1980).
6. Majka and Majka, *Farm Workers,* pp. 158–66; Acuña, *Occupied America,* pp. 144–50; García, *Operation Wetback,* pp. 45–57; Ellis W. Hawley, "The Politics of the

Mexican Labor Issue, 1950–1965," *Agricultural History* 40 (1966): 157–76; Galarza, *Merchants of Labor,* pp. 183–98; California Senate, Committee on Labor and Welfare, *California's Farm Labor Problems* (Sacramento, CA: Senate of the State of California, 1961); Tony Dunbar and Linda Kravitz, *Hard Traveling: Migrant Farm Workers in America* (Cambridge, MA: Ballinger Publishing, 1976), pp. 69–98; Miles Corwin, "The Grapes of Wrath Revisited," *Los Angeles Times,* September 29, 1991.

7. Martínez, *Border People,* pp. 148–55.

8. Ted Conover, Coyotes: *A Journey through the Secret World of America's Illegal Aliens* (New York: Vintage Books, 1987).

9. Quoted in Jones, *Ambivalent Journey,* pp. 100–102.

10. J. Cockroft, *Outlaws in the Promised Land,* p. 109.

11. Lorey, *United States-Mexico Border Statistics since 1900,* Table 1011.

12. Tamayo and Fernández, *Zonas fronterizas,* p. 37.

13. See Martínez, *Border Boom Town;* and Thurber D. Profitt, "The Symbiotic Frontier: The Emergence of Tijuana since 1769" (Ph.D. diss., UCLA, 1988).

14. U.S. International Trade Commission, *The Impact of Increased United States-Mexico Trade on Southwest Border Development* (Washington, DC: Government Printing Office, 1986); Paul Ganster, "Percepciones de la migración mexicana en el condado de San Diego," *Revista Mexicana de Sociología* 53 (1991): 259–90; Ganster, "Impact of the Peso's Devaluation on Retail Sales in San Diego County," *San Diego Economic Bulletin* 33 (March 1985).

15. Hansen, *The Border Economy,* p. 37. See also Mayo Murrieta and Alberto Hernando, *Puente México: La vecindad de Tijuana con California* (Tijuana: Colegio de la Frontera Norte, 1991).

16. Martínez, *Border People,* pp. 277–83.

17. Timothy C. Brown, "The Fourth Member of NAFTA: The U.S.-Mexico Border," *Annals of the American Academy of Political and Social Science* 550 (March 1997): 115, 116.

18. See also Lorey, *United States-Mexico Border Statistics since 1900,* Table 2010, which shows that per capita income in the Mexican border region was significantly higher than the national average in 1980.

19. Quoted in Martínez, *Border Boom Town,* p. 109.

20. Quoted in ibid.

21. See also Lorey, *United States-Mexico Border Statistics since 1900,* Tables 315, 316.

22. Pan-American Health Organization (PAHO) *U.S.-Mexico Border Health Statistics,* 6th ed. (El Paso, TX: PAHO, 1990).

23. United Nations, *Evolución de la frontera norte,* p. 63.

24. Martín de la Rosa, *La presencia de grupos norteamericanos en Tijuana* (Tijuana: Colegio de la Frontera Norte, 1987), chap. 1; José Manuel Valenzuela Arce, *El movimiento urbano popular en Tijuana* (Tijuana: Colegio de la Frontera Norte, 1987), p. 13.

25. PAHO, *U.S.-Mexico Border Health Statistics.*

26. José Manuel Valenzuela Arce, *Empapados de sereno: El movimiento urbano popular en Baja California (1928–1988)* (Tijuana: El Colegio de la Frontera Norte, 1991).

27. When interpreting the data in Table 6-5 it is important to consider the fact that because the categories employed to define Mexican-origin population differed in several census years, they are not strictly comparable from one year to another.

28. Ganster and Sweedler, "The United States-Mexico Border Region," p. 423.

29. U.S. Bureau of the Census, unpublished data (U.S. Department of Commerce, Washington, DC, 1990). Data refer to population aged five and over.

30. Martínez, *Border People.*

31. See Walter Fogel, *Mexican Americans in Southwest Labor Markets* (Los Angeles: Mexican-American Study Project, University of California, 1967), pp. 7–21, 145–69; U.S. Department of Commerce, Bureau of the Census, *Current Population Reports—Demographic, Social, and Economic Profile of States: Spring 1976,* Series P-20, #334 (Washington, DC: Government Printing Office, 1979), p. 47; National Commission for Employment Policy, *Hispanics and Jobs: Barriers to Progress* (Washington, DC: National Commission for Employment Policy, 1982), pp. 45–56; California Department of Industrial Relations, *Californians of Spanish Surname* (San Francisco: California Department of Industrial Relations, 1964), pp. 17–18, 33, 46–52.

32. See Lorey, *United States-Mexico Border Statistics since 1900: 1990 Update,* Table 711.

33. "Latinos Lead Southern California's Economic Boom," *Statesman-Journal* (Oregon), July 18, 1997. The article was based on a *Washington Post* story.

34. Massey, "March of Folly," p. 16.

35. Jones, *Ambivalent Journey,* pp. 95–96.

36. See J. Edward Taylor, "International-Migrant Remittances, Savings, and Development in Migrant-Sending Areas" (paper prepared for the International Migration at Century's End conference, Barcelona, Spain, May 7–10, 1997); and Ricardo Sandoval, "Migrants Fueling Ventures in Mexico," *San Jose Mercury News,* June 29, 1998.

37. Jones, *Ambivalent Journey,* pp. 105–6.

38. J. Edward Taylor, "Mexico-to-U.S. Migration and Rural Mexico: A Village Economy-wide Perspective," in *Immigration and Ethnic Communities: A Focus on Latinos,* ed. Refugio I. Rochín (East Lansing: Julian Samora Research Institute, Michigan State University, 1996), pp. 59–66.

39. Rodolfo de la Garza et al., "Binational Impact of Latino Remittances" (policy brief [of the Tomás Rivera Policy Institute], March 1997).

40. See two excellent chapters in Ross, *Views across the Border:* Carlos Monsiváis, "The Culture of the Frontier: The Mexican Side," pp. 50–67; and Américo Paredes, "The Problem of Identity in a Changing Culture: Popular Expressions of Culture Conflict along the Lower Rio Grande Border," pp. 68–94. See also David R. Maciel and María Herrera-Sobek, eds., *Culture across Borders: Mexican Immigration and Popular Culture* (Tucson: University of Arizona Press, 1998); and Jorge A. Bustamante, "Demystifying the United States-Mexico Border," *Journal of American History* 79 (1992): 485–90.

41. Tinker Salas, *In the Shadow of the Eagles,* p. 149.

42. Ibid., pp. 145, 258.

43. Ibid., p. 118.

44. Ibid., p. 150. See also Josiah McC. Heyman, "Imports and Standards of Justice on the Mexico-United States Border," in *The Allure of the Foreign: Imported Goods in Postcolonial Latin America,* ed. Benjamin Orlove (Ann Arbor: University of Michigan Press, 1997), pp. 151–83.

45. Tinker Salas, *In the Shadow of the Eagles,* p. 31.

46. Manuel Peña, "Música Fronteriza/Border Music" (manuscript, n.p., n.d.).

47. See David Reyes and Tom Waldman, *Land of a Thousand Dances: Chicano Rock 'n Roll from Southern California* (Albuquerque: University of New Mexico Press, 1998) and companion CD set *Brown-Eyed Soul* (Rhino Records); Steven Loza, *Barrio Rhythm: Mexican American Music in Los Angeles* (Urbana: University of Illinois Press, 1992); Américo Paredes, *A Texas-Mexican "Cancionero": Folksongs of the Lower Rio Grande Border* (Urbana: University of Illinois Press, 1976); Américo Paredes, "The Mexican Corrido: Its Rise and Fall," in *Madstones and Twisters,* ed. Moody C. Boatright (Dallas: Publications of the Texas Folklore Society, 1958), pp. 91–105; Manuel Peña, *The Texas-Mexican Conjunto: History of a Working Class Music* (Austin: University of Texas Press, 1985); and Manuel Peña, "Music for a Changing Community: Three Generations of a Chicano Family *Orquesta,*" *Latin American Music Review* 8 (1987): 230–45.

48. See Jean Charlot, *Mexican Mural Renaissance* (New Haven: Yale University Press, 1963); Eva Cockcroft, John Weber, and James Cockcroft, *Towards a People's Art: The Contemporary Mural Movement* (New York: E. P. Dutton, 1977); and Jacinto Quirarte, "Chicano Murals in San Diego," in *Reglas del juego y juego sin reglas en la vida fronteriza/Rules of the Game and Games without Rules in Border Life,* ed. Mario Miranda and James W. Wilkie (Mexico, D.F.: Asociación Nacional de Universidades e Institutos de Enseñanza Superior, 1985), pp. 229–54.

49. David R. Maciel, "Braceros, Mayordomos, and Alambristas: Mexican Immigration to the United States in Contemporary Cinema," *Hispanic Journal of Behavioral Sciences* 8 (1986): 371–72.

50. Norma Iglesias, *Entre yerba, polvo y plomo: Lo fronterizo visto por el cine mexicano* (Tijuana: Colegio de la Frontera Norte, 1991); David R. Maciel, *El Norte: The U.S.-Mexican Border in Contemporary Cinema* (San Diego: Institute for Regional Studies of the Californias, San Diego State University, 1990); Carl J. Mora, *Mexican Cinema: Reflections of a Society, 1896–1980* (Berkeley: University of California Press, 1982); and Allen L. Woll, *The Latin Image in American Film,* rev. ed. (Los Angeles: UCLA Latin American Center Publications, 1980).

51. See, for example, Edward Simmen, ed., *North of the Rio Grande: The Mexican-American Experience in Short Fiction* (New York: Penguin, 1992).

52. See, for example, José Manuel Di-Bella, Sergio Gómez Montro, and Harry Polkinhorn, eds., *Literatura de la frontera México-Estados Unidos: Memoria del primer encuentro de escritores de las Californias/Mexican-American Border Writing: Proceedings of the First Conference of Writers from the Californias* (Mexicali/San Diego: Dirección de Asuntos Culturales de la Secretaría de Educación y Bienestar Social del Gobierno del Estado de Baja California/Institute for Regional Studies of the Californias, San Diego State University, 1987).

53. See, for example, Héctor Calderón and José David Saldívar, eds., *Criticism in the Borderlands: Studies in Chicano Literature, Culture, and Ideology* (Durham, NC:

Duke University Press, 1991); José E. Limón, *Mexican Ballads, Chicano Poems: History and Influence in Mexican-American Social Poetry* (Berkeley: University of California Press, 1992); and Gloria Anzaldúa, *Making Faces, Making Souls— Haciendo Caras: Creative and Critical Perspectives by Women of Color* (San Francisco: Aunt Lute Foundation Books, 1990).

CHAPTER SEVEN | # U.S.-MEXICAN RELATIONS AT THE BORDER

1890s TO 1990s

THE ECONOMIC AND SOCIAL TRENDS that defined the border region in the twentieth century show all signs of continuing unbroken into the twenty-first. As the area evolves, it will continue to play an ever more important role in the social and economic lives of the people of Mexico and the United States. Undoubtedly, the border will also figure ever more prominently in the interactions between the two countries and their inhabitants. Issues in U.S.-Mexican relations—economic, social, political, and strategic—have often been most pronounced, and most divisive, along the boundary. There, domestic and international issues come face to face and exert a constant influence on one another. Consideration of bilateral relations is most useful in the context of long-term historical changes in the border region since 1900, for the historical record provides a portent of things to come.

THE ELUSIVE BOUNDARY:
WATER, ENVIRONMENTAL ISSUES,
AND DRUG TRAFFICKING

Relations between Mexico and the United States have often focused directly on the boundary that unites and divides the two countries. The U.S.-Mexican border was arbitrarily drawn in much of the natural terrain through which it cuts, a fact that has had a lasting impact on regional conflicts. Such natural resources as water and such environmental problems as air pollution, which have never paid much attention to the location of the international boundary, have become binational problems spanning the border.

The fact that the physical boundary was not only drawn in an arbitrary fashion but has also moved in the relatively recent past has generated serious tensions between Mexico and the United States. Beginning in the late nineteenth century, conflict between the United States and Mexico repeatedly came to a head over such issues as the shifting of the Rio Grande/Río Bravo boundary and the division of the waters of the Colorado River for irrigation on both sides of the border. Conceptions of the border also changed over time. The maritime boundaries between the United States and Mexico at the border, for example, proved to be a continual source of friction in the 1980s and 1990s, as the Mexican fishing industry boomed and environmentalists concerned about dolphin kills achieved an embargo on Mexican tuna imports.[1]

Among the most complex disputes over the physical boundary was that of the Chamizal, a 600-acre tract of land adjacent to the Rio Grande in the vicinity of El Paso and Ciudad Juárez. At the time of the signing of the Treaty of Guadalupe Hidalgo in 1848, the Chamizal was south of the Rio Grande in Mexico. But flooding led to changes in the river's course, and by 1864 the tract was north of the river in the United States. For residents of Ciudad Juárez and the state of Chihuahua, the Chamizal remained national territory, and they denounced U.S. claims to jurisdiction over the area. Although the central government of Mexico formally protested in 1867, neither nation assigned the matter a high priority, and it remained unresolved—and frequently a thorn in international relations—until the midtwentieth century. It was not until 1963, when U.S.-Mexican relations reached a high watermark fueled by U.S. concerns about the Cuban revolution, that the Chamizal territory was returned to Mexico.

The dispute over the Chamizal was not the only one caused by changes in the Rio Grande's course. Morteritos Island, near Roma, Texas, was part of Mexico until 1884, when Texans claimed jurisdiction because in 1848 the island was on the U.S. side of the river. Additional disagreements arising from the shifting course of the Rio Grande prompted the United States and Mexico to sign a treaty in 1884 providing for negotiated settlements over lands transferred from one side of the border to the other in this way. Five years later the responsibility for administering the treaty was placed in the hands of an International Boundary Commission, which has managed the transfer of hundreds of acres of land along the Rio Grande/Río Bravo during the last century.

In a region where water constitutes the lifeblood of both urban and rural existence, it is not surprising that the flow of the Colorado River became a source of lasting conflict between the two countries. Toward the end of the nineteenth century, as population increased along the border and in the adjacent states, U.S. entrepreneurs began building irrigation works north of the boundary, which reduced the amount of water entering the Mexican border states. In 1895, Mexico filed a 35-million-dollar claim with the International Boundary Commission. The commission urged the two countries to negotiate a comprehensive treaty regulating the use of water for irrigation. But settlement of the dispute would not come until 1922, when U.S. state representatives signed the Colorado River Compact, which divided the river into two basins, each with rights to half the water. Two years later, Mexico and the United States signed a treaty guaranteeing Mexico 1.5 million acre-feet per year.

Conflicts over the Colorado's water intensified in the 1940s and 1950s, as infrastructure investment in agricultural production soared in both countries. The International Boundary and Water Commission was established in 1944 to continue the work of the International Boundary Commission and to address water quality issues. By the 1960s, water flowing to

An aerial view of agricultural fields at Mexicali-Calexico
shows the uneven nature of water distribution.
David E. Lorey

the delta in the Gulf of California—on the Mexican side of the border—
had ceased entirely. Mexico filed complaints with the United States about
both the amount and the quality of water it received. In 1973 the dispute
over the Colorado was finally resolved through agreements on the amount
of water that would be available to the Mexican side of the border and
the levels of salinity that would be acceptable for the water delivered (the
water-treatment plant called for in the agreements did not actually begin
operations until years later). Pressures caused by the precious flow of the
Colorado are certain to continue. The Colorado now supplies water to eight
border states and at least twenty million users. In 1997 a new U.S. ruling
divided the Colorado's water among the western states and allowed for the
sale of excess stored water by some states to Nevada and California, which
are always in need of more than their allocated share (both San Diego and
Tijuana import about 85 percent of their water).

Similar battles raged over the waters of the Rio Grande/Río Bravo, which
separates the U.S. border states of New Mexico and Texas both from one
another and from the Mexican states of Tamaulipas and Nuevo León. In
1938 a treaty was signed in the United States to apportion Rio Grande water
among U.S. border states. The 1944 water treaty with Mexico established
rules for sharing the bounty of the lower Rio Grande, and two reservoirs—
the Falcón and the Amistad—were built to control water flow. But as population grew in the postwar period, these agreements were no longer
satisfactory for managing water in the region. The states of Tamaulipas and
Nuevo León tangled over the thorny issue of urban and industrial water
needs in Monterrey versus agricultural water needs in Tamaulipas. Texas
and New Mexico found themselves with entirely different legal conceptions of water rights. For all states concerned, the lack of attention to
groundwater resources and their interconnection with surface flows meant
that water issues were far from resolved. Similarly, Mexico and the United
States had never signed a bilateral groundwater treaty.

According to several mid-1990s reports from the Mexican government
and multilateral organizations, Mexico's shortage of fresh water in the North
was caused by overexploitation of existing aquifers and a lack of adequate
infrastructure for water treatment and distribution. A 1997 World Bank

report announced that almost one-third of Mexico's 258 aquifers were in danger of running dry. The threat of water shortages was greatest in sixteen states in northwestern, northern, and central Mexico. It was estimated that the aquifer underlying Ciudad Juárez-El Paso was being drained at an unsustainable twenty times the rate of recharge; at that pace, the water supply would be exhausted by 2025. Conflicts over both surface and subsurface water showed no sign of abating. As groundwater sources were depleted and both groundwater and coastal areas became polluted, water issues were more likely than ever to continue to plague U.S.-Mexican relations at the border.

Water shortages increased vulnerability to contamination from toxic substances and salt water. Untreated industrial and municipal wastes were discharged into the waterways on both sides of the border, contaminating aquifers throughout the region. One of the best examples of pollution is the Salton Sea, the body of water lying just north of the international boundary in California. Without drainage to the sea, the levels of contaminants in the Salton Sea—mostly caused by agricultural runoff containing both naturally occurring substances and fertilizer, herbicide, and pesticide residues from Mexico and the United States—made the lake a toxic stew. The New River, actually a drainage ditch originating in Mexicali, added human wastes to the Salton Sea. Huge numbers of migratory seabirds, including the endangered California brown pelican, died off in 1996 and 1997, and the threat to nearby human populations became increasingly serious. In many areas along the border the quality of groundwater deteriorated as a result of agricultural runoff laden with salts and chemical residues, effluent from leaking industrial storage tanks, and seepage from solid-waste disposal sites.

Water pollution led to health threats on both sides of the border, as in the case of the untreated sewage that flowed north from Tijuana to San Diego. Not until 1997 did an international joint sewage-treatment plant on the California side of the border begin operations, and its capacity was quickly overwhelmed. A plant in Tijuana was able to treat only about one-half of the waste it received and provided only primary treatment of sewage. In the Texas *colonias* along the Rio Grande, hepatitis occurred at several times the national average.[2] A mysterious epidemic of spina bifida and anencephaly, both neural-tube defects, swept the Texas border counties between 1988 and 1992, affecting children at more than twice the average U.S. rate. Although many observers suspected toxic chemical exposure related to *maquiladora* employment, the link was not proven.[3] One of the growth industries on the border much criticized by environmentalists and public-health experts alike was the industrial processing of hazardous waste for use as fuel. Landfill projects for hazardous-waste interment also sparked fears of water contamination.

Hardly restricted to water, environmental degradation was a pervasive problem that involved various interrelated forces on both sides of the border. The by-products of the occasional U.S. businesses that managed to escape stringent environmental regulations in the United States[4] were accompanied by the more general environmental fallout from rapid industrialization and population growth in the border region.[5] Foul air north and south of the boundary was generated by automobiles, smelting plants and other businesses, and agriculture (through smoke from burning fields and dust storms from overtilled soil). The mixing and movement of pollutants in air currents—stemming from different sources in Mexico and the United States—created a regionwide problem, particularly severe in Ciudad Juárez-El Paso and Tijuana-San Diego.

Lack of data and control mechanisms exacerbated environmental problems at the border. Many *maquiladoras* had toxic-discharge problems, according to the Mexican government.[6] In the mid-1980s it was estimated that forty-four tons of hazardous *maquila* waste per day went unaccounted for. In the 1990s the problem persisted—only 12 percent of *maquiladoras* were estimated to achieve compliance with hazardous-material regulations requiring the return of substances to the United States for processing and disposal.[7]

Attempts to clean up the border environment or stop further degradation, although erratic, left some room for hope. Even though their efforts were hampered by the lack of legal integration between the United States and Mexico, policymakers found themselves forced by the pressing nature of environmental problems and their political volatility to take action.

In 1992, as part of the push for NAFTA, President George Bush and President Carlos Salinas de Gortari formulated an Integrated Environmental Plan for the U.S.-Mexican border that they hoped would end environmentalists' opposition to their proposed free-trade agreement. The United States was to contribute 384 million dollars and Mexico 460 million dollars to the three-year program. The 1997 completion of the long-awaited binational wastewater treatment plant at the Tijuana-San Diego border, even if its accomplishments proved to be limited, was also an important milestone in transboundary cooperation for environmental planning. In these enforcement and cleanup programs the difficulties involved in monitoring the use and transport of both human and industrial waste created major obstacles. Sewage treatment was nonexistent on most of the Mexican side of the border, and the law concerning the tracking of industrial waste across the international border was unclear. Much hazardous waste remained in inadequate temporary storage at production sites, where it posed a major health risk to local residents.

With the signing of NAFTA in 1993 a side agreement on environmental issues was initiated in the hope of slowing degradation and protecting the health of border residents. But both the Border Environmental Cooperation Commission (BECC) and the North American Development Bank (NADBank)—the two agencies charged with border environmental improvement under NAFTA—moved slowly during their early years. NADBank, headquartered in San Antonio, was to make loans to border cities to fund such projects as water-purification and sewage-treatment plants. The role of BECC, established in Ciudad Juárez, was to evaluate and certify border environmental infrastructure projects as necessary and viable, a status required for consideration for NADBank loans. BECC soon became bogged down in administrative red tape, including a contentious selection process for its director; NADBank found that the border communities most needful of environmental infrastructure lacked the wherewithal to secure or repay loans, a situation that worsened after the peso devaluation of 1994–95. NADBank was restricted from directly funding cleanup (the cost of which was estimated by some environmentalists at 30 billion dollars) and from addressing pollution problems at their source. At the national level the U.S. Environmental Protection Agency set up an office in El Paso, and legislation was passed in the U.S. Congress to create a Border Environmental Health Laboratory there as well. Once again, however, few short-term accomplishments inspired confidence in the will or ability of politicians to deliver concrete long-term environmental solutions.

In the 1980s, drug trafficking reemerged as a pressing issue in border life, broadly affecting U.S.-Mexican relations as well as the regional economy and society. The United States blamed Mexico for its role as the source of the illegal drugs and for its failure to prevent the drugs from being transshipped through the border region to the United States. Indeed, Mexico had clearly come to supplant Colombia in the U.S.-Latin American drug trade; Andean countries controlled the production and Colombia controlled the refining of cocaine, but Mexican drug lords dominated distribution and marketing in the United States. One analyst estimated that, in 1984, Mexico was the source of 36 percent of the heroin, 30 percent of the cocaine, and 9 percent of the marijuana sold in the United States.[8]

Mexico countered such charges by arguing that its extensive drug interdiction programs could not change the fact that the U.S. market represented the principal stimulant to drug trafficking. U.S. consumers continued to spend in excess of 50 billion dollars per year on illegal drugs. Thirty-four percent of the total population aged twelve and older in the United States had used illegal drugs. In Mexico only 3.9 percent of the equivalent population had experimented with drugs. Domestic production of marijuana in California, Kentucky, and Tennessee probably accounted for one-half of U.S. consumption.[9] The heated exchanges between U.S. and Mexican spokespeople on the drug issue were reminiscent of the Prohibition years, when illegal substances had similarly shaped border life and affected international relations.

Just as during Prohibition, the trade in illegal substances was both a boon and a bane for border communities. It brought benefits to some individuals and to some local communities, providing jobs and investment capital and stimulating local markets for a broad array of legal as well as illegal goods and services. But regional social costs—violence abetted by high-tech weaponry, organized crime, corruption of local officials, addiction, and health problems (including HIV infection) from Los Angeles to Mexico City—far outweighed the benefits. The drug malaise spread like a cancer from the border nexus. Gangs involved in the trade and its associated service industries routinely crossed the border to engage in illegal activities and escape detection and prosecution.

By the late 1980s the concern over the trade in illegal drugs led the United States to station the National Guard at the international boundary; by the 1990s there was widespread fear that the border would be militarized in order to control the flow of drugs and migrants. In 1997 the U.S. Department of Defense, responding to an outcry against the use of the military in drug-trafficking assignments along the U.S.-Mexican border, ordered U.S. ground-troop units to halt foot patrols in the region. The action was a clear result of the heavy criticism from citizens and officials in Texas and Mexico following an incident in which a U.S. Marine shot an eighteen-year-old high-school student along the Texas border. The two hundred or so soldiers and U.S. Marines supporting overall U.S. antidrug efforts at the border were withdrawn.[10]

MIGRATION

Migration has been one of the longest-lasting and most sensitive border issues for Mexico and the United States. A host of concerns raised by legal and illegal immigration to the United States from Mexico, and the status and treatment of legal and illegal residents of the border region, have time and again been at the center of conflict between the two countries. The migration debate has pitted citizens of Mexico against citizens of the United States and citizens of the United States against one another.

The immigration "problem" is a creation of the twentieth century. From 1848 until the end of the nineteenth century, the border was not patrolled and migration across it concerned few people. Early U.S. immigration legislation (in 1917 and 1924) generally made exceptions for Mexican migrants; only in 1929 did it become a crime to enter the United States from Mexico without documentation.

The tensions caused by the migration issue as we now think of it emerged in the 1940s with the institutionalized flow of Mexican temporary workers under the Bracero agreement, as U.S. farmers sought Mexican labor during the peak of the wartime economic boom. The Bracero Program instituted a network throughout Mexico, at the border, and in the United States that both stimulated and facilitated migration for seasonal or permanent employment in the United States. U.S. economic expansion in the postwar period was concentrated in the states where migrant networks were most ingrained. Jobs in cities—and in services—became more common, and this employment was generally not seasonal in nature. As a result, migration became more permanent and increasingly characterized by the movement of families rather than of individual males. The flow of migrants became dizzyingly diverse, consisting of many groups moving for many different reasons.

Once a network was established and family members were in place to provide communications and assistance, the migrant flow could not simply be shut off whenever the United States economy cooled down. The fact that migrant populations from Mexico had historically been recognized and accepted as U.S. citizens after a period of work and acculturation, regardless of reforms in U.S. immigration laws, reinforced migration networks and migrant lore.[11]

The northward flow of workers became increasingly considered illegal as U.S. immigration law changed. The 1965 amendments to the Immigration and Nationality Act eliminated national-origin quotas. Coming as it did at the end of the Bracero Program, this reform (and further modifications of the law in 1976) converted the status of a large portion of the long-established Mexican migrant flow from legal to illegal. Ironically, with these changes in immigration law, the debate over migrant labor switched from a traditional focus on quotas for legal immigrants to concerns about illegal immigrants.

The fate of the much debated Immigration Reform and Control Act of 1986 (IRCA) proved that the immigration dilemma was not easily solved. After a brief three-year period during which the promulgation of the act seemed to slow border crossings, migration climbed to its previous levels.

The act also sent mixed signals to potential migrants by creating a framework for the legalization of the status of millions of Mexicans who had been living illegally in the United States; by the fall of 1988 some 3.1 million had applied for amnesty.[12]

A large body of recent research conducted by experts on migration issues indicates that both Mexico and the United States have probably gained more than they have lost from the northward flow of Mexican people in the period between 1940 and 1995.[13] Some immigrants were clearly net beneficiaries of certain U.S. public services (notably primary and middle-school education), but in general those costs were more than recouped in the form of benefits to hundreds of thousands of employers (who profited by paying low wages) as well as to millions of consumers (who benefited from paying low prices).

Several findings of the new literature on immigration refute widely held beliefs.[14] Migration from Mexico, for example, correlated much more strongly with U.S. employment needs than with Mexican unemployment. And the principal benefit to employers of migrant labor was not its low cost but its flexibility. Many recent studies do not detect any statistically significant difference between the characteristics of legal and illegal migrants: age, family status, education, English proficiency, and income were more important than legal status in determining how Mexican migrants affected the U.S. economy, whether they stayed, how well they assimilated, and how they fared economically.[15] The assimilation of new arrivals from Mexico was as fast as or faster than that of other migrant groups: 90 percent of first-generation Hispanics born in California had native fluency in English; in the second generation only 50 percent still spoke Spanish.[16]

The net fiscal benefit to the United States and Mexico also appeared to be positive. Although some states, such as California and Texas, and gateway cities, such as Los Angeles and New York, incurred substantial net fiscal costs for migration, the national advantage outweighed the difference. This situation, however, rendered the allocation of tax resources a major source of conflict between state and local governments on the one hand and the federal government on the other. For the Mexican economy, immigrants' remittances to family members became one of the major sources of foreign exchange—roughly as important as tourism or manufactured exports.

The causes of migration proved to be much more complex than had earlier been believed. Far more important for migrants than the simple push-and-pull factors of wage differentials were larger, global issues of market consolidation (including North American integration), the process of learning that accrues to migrants (sometimes called human capital), and the networks created by migration (sometimes referred to as social capital). Consequently, migrants generally came not from poor, isolated communities disconnected from international markets but from areas undergoing rapid change as the result of insertion into global production networks. Migrants sought not income, but investment capital and insurance against risk in their communities of origin.[17]

The problems with migration, according to new studies, were primarily concerned with its contribution to continuing poverty. Migrants tended to

The U.S. Border Patrol stops to watch a soccer game played by
Mexican youths on the U.S. side of the border, where the field is flat.
After dark the game becomes more serious.
David E. Lorey

Migrants at the border wait for nightfall.
David E. Lorey

depress the wages of low-skilled U.S. workers, for example, particularly the 10 percent of the U.S. work force with fewer than twelve years of education. And migrants themselves—again those with the least schooling—sometimes remained mired in poverty, forcing them to rely on public assistance in the United States.[18] In times of economic downturn, migrants suffered the brunt of concerns over scarce jobs. In California in the early 1990s, for example, voters passed a series of laws to exclude migrants from public benefits. Migrant life also remained insecure: in 1996 and 1997, changes in U.S. enforcement led to a series of deaths, as migrants were compelled to reroute their journeys northward and cross through less-hospitable border terrain.

Many migration experts supported alternative approaches to the largely ineffectual, periodic policy tightening and border-crossing enforcement. The policies had not generally been logical responses to the deep-level causes and consequences of migration but rather short-term reactions driven by debates that were locked in outdated understandings of the phenomenon. In general, the experts believed, U.S. policies based in efforts to drive up the cost of migrating actually lowered the odds of repatriation and increased the numbers of permanent undocumented residents, converting a circular movement into a unidirectional flow.[19] Some specialists believed that annual quotas or formal guest-worker programs would be more successful solutions to what was seen as the ongoing immigration problem.

Regardless of scholarly assessments of the meanings and impacts of migration from Mexico, historically the flow has been accompanied by acrimonious debate over both its short-term and long-term economic and social effects. In the United States many agribusiness, manufacturing, and service employers of migrants—legal and illegal—argued for easy access to inexpensive Mexican labor. Organized labor, in contrast, argued that low wage rates put U.S. workers out of jobs. Many residents of the United States felt that, by allowing or implicitly encouraging Mexican migration, the United States was losing control of its borders and thus of its sovereignty. Further complicating the picture was the importance of the migration "safety valve" to Mexican political stability, which was a prime concern for U.S. national security.

Adding to the difficulty of understanding illegal immigration to the United States from Mexico was the inability to measure the flow accurately.[20] Problems in INS data collection—such as the fact that the same individuals were sometimes counted repeatedly and that the number of aliens seized rose when the INS and the border patrol received increased funding—kept policymakers in the dark about the real dimensions of migration. And the changing dynamics and dimensions of migration, which might have had a major impact on policy, were little understood: migrants increasingly came from urban rather than rural areas, they more often sought manufacturing and service employment instead of agricultural work, they more frequently came to the U.S. border states intending to stay permanently, and more women and families joined the flow.

The continuing flow of immigrants across the porous boundary and into the border region was from time to time accompanied by hostility and by heightened tensions in the bilateral relationship. Periodic bouts of violence against immigrants at the hands of the U.S. Border Patrol, proven or alleged, received much media attention and led Mexico to lodge formal complaints

The thoroughly contained border at Ciudad Juárez-El Paso
proves no match for daily crossers in the background.
David E. Lorey

with the United States and to include the issue in discussions between Mexican and U.S. presidents.[21] With each attempt to crack down on migrants—for example, the mid-1990s initiatives known as Operation Hold the Line in El Paso and Operation Gatekeeper at the San Ysidro border crossing—U.S.-Mexican relations suffered. Mexico charged that its citizens were physically mistreated, deprived of food and water, kept in crowded jail cells, and denied first aid after apprehension by the border patrol. These measures disrupted local economies but seemed to have little effect on long-distance migrants, who simply crossed the border at other places. Ironically, stepped-up enforcement discouraged migrants from returning to Mexico.

Available data clearly suggest that the United States will be unable to stop the movement of people northward as long as North American economic integration continues, migrant networks exist to direct the flow and allocate jobs and the communities sending migrants need their remittances for investment and insurance purposes. It is not clear that immigration law reforms in 1986 and 1996 or militarization of the border have succeeded in appreciably slowing the flow; in fact they have sometimes encouraged migrants to stay in the United States. It seems safe to predict that migration will continue to haunt U.S.-Mexican relations and debate over the issue will continue to shape life in the border region.

NAFTA IN THE BORDER REGION

By the 1990s the economies above and below the international boundary had become more closely intertwined than at any earlier time. Awareness of this economic integration was greatly enhanced by the debate over NAFTA and its passage by the U.S. Congress in November 1993. Ironically—given the spirited debate that preceded the congressional vote—the agreement introduced no fundamental changes to the U.S.-Mexican relationship; the border is the best proof of this fact. What NAFTA did was to establish a framework to facilitate and regulate future commercial and financial flows in North America.[22]

Free trade was the economic policy in Mexico that brought the reforms of Salinas (during his presidency from 1988 to 1994) to the attention of the international community. By spearheading NAFTA, Salinas went forward with the opening of the Mexican economy begun during the de la Madrid administration (1982–1988) as a response to the economic crisis of the 1980s. The Mexican government's approach to reactivating the economy—which had been hit by a sharp decline in the price of oil and peaking interest rates—was to privatize state-owned companies and facilitate foreign competition and investment in the country. From the mid-1980s, Mexico substantially reduced its tariff rates, amending its laws and its constitution to spur foreign investment. Tariffs that averaged 24 percent in 1984 dropped to 11 percent by 1990. In a 1986 policy shift as important as the signing of NAFTA, Mexico committed itself to freer world trade by joining the General Agreement on Tariffs and Trade (GATT). In his pursuit of free trade with the United States, Salinas was responding to the desperate need for investment in a context in which neither oil nor loans could be counted on to fuel Mexican development. Mexican domestic economic policy drove the free-trade initiative.

Debate over the establishment of a formal free-trade area raged for the three years between 1990 and 1993, and then there was another one-to-two-year wait to see what NAFTA would mean. Nevertheless, the interdependence of the U.S. and Mexican economies had been a historical fact for at least a century. As already shown, the pace of economic integration of the two countries had increased markedly after World War II until, by the 1980s, Mexico had become the third-largest trading partner of the United States. The border region was particularly closely incorporated into the binational economy; in 1900, for example, one-third of Texas's exports went to Mexico.

There were several areas in which scholars agreed substantially on the meaning of freer trade for the border region. First was the issue of job creation, loss, and transfer. There was widespread fear that NAFTA would spur a massive relocation of U.S. factory jobs to Mexico. But this concern was based on a gross exaggeration of the role of labor in production costs and location decisions and an underestimation of the expense involved in building new factories and training new workers in Mexico. As many economists pointed out, jobs would be created by the volume and vigor of overall trade; if commerce grew in a balanced way on both sides (which freer trade made more likely), employment would increase in both countries.

Trends after 1994 bore out these assessments. The focus on manufacturing was the central flaw in the argument that free trade would be followed by a general relocation of industrial jobs from the United States to Mexico. From the outset of the debate the biggest impact of NAFTA was certain to be in areas other than manufacturing. The attention on jobs in such industries as steel, autos, textiles, and appliances was generally misplaced. The real action was certain to be in the service sector, which was more important to all three NAFTA-related North American economies (U.S., Mexican, and Canadian) than agriculture and manufacturing combined. Sure enough, the biggest growth areas in the first few years of NAFTA were such services as retailing, banking, communications, transportation, insurance, publishing, tourism, film distribution, educational civil engineering, software design, and natural gas and electric-power distribution. Because these industries were previously off limits to U.S. capital, such new investments in Mexico implied few if any lost jobs in the United States.

A second fear about NAFTA involved wages: one-dollar-per-hour wages in Mexico would surely take jobs from U.S. workers who were paid much more. But there were many questionable assumptions behind this concern. The commonly cited one-dollar-per-hour pay scales, for example, were atypical in Mexican manufacturing; the infamous 10-to-1 wage figures were derived from misleading GDP-per-capita comparisons. Economists pointed out that a better measure would be GDP per industrial worker. There the ratio was 2 to 1, and it represented the average difference between Mexican and U.S. productivity in advanced industrial installations, which, of course, wages can be expected to reflect. U.S. firms might be able to pay employees half as much, but the workers would then only produce about half as much in the same time. Mexican productivity was low because of poor education, obsolete technology, and inefficient management. Many economists also pointed out that low wages were not the key to future Mexican industrial strength. Mexico's future manufacturing success would depend instead on a whole host of factors, in particular the ability to develop and adapt new technologies and design new products. In modern manufacturing, labor costs generally represent a low proportion of the total value added.

A central issue often overlooked in the jobs-and-wages debate was infrastructure. Even with low wages it frequently cost much more to produce goods in Mexico than in the United States. Electricity was more expensive; railroads were less efficient; roads and ports were in disrepair. And there were additional costs of production—such as benefits, training, and turnover rates—at least as important as wages in influencing location decisions. The fact that there was no great rush to move manufacturing jobs to Mexico after NAFTA went into effect indicates that firms were aware of these issues and accustomed to taking them into account in their decision making.

Other fears about NAFTA revolved around migration. Some supporters believed that NAFTA would eventually attract U.S. industry to Mexico,

Trucks wait to bring merchandise across the border
at the Nuevo Laredo-Laredo crossing.
Paul Ganster, Institute for Regional Studies of the Californias

revitalizing Mexico's economy and putting its people to work at home rather than forcing them to seek employment in the United States. This idea, however, was anathema to U.S. organized labor, already distraught because of declining influence and membership (which had fallen from a high of 22,025,000 members in 1979 to 16,740,000 by 1990) and worried that U.S. industries would leave the country and Mexican migrants would drive wages down. These fears, although widespread, were not borne out by data on the first several years of life under NAFTA.[23] Serious students of demography did not expect NAFTA to show any effect on migration trends—which were entrenched in patterns of U.S.-Mexican interdependence going back half a century—for some five to ten years.

Preliminary data on NAFTA trade outcomes made some observers' early fears appear overblown. Total bilateral trade soared to 150 billion dollars per year from the 35-billion-dollar annual pace of 1987. In the first six months of 1994, commerce grew by 20 percent over the previous year (about three times as fast as overall export growth in the period). Throughout the 1990s, U.S.-Mexican trade increased at 25 percent per year. Although U.S. exports to Mexico fell in 1995, they were still greater than in 1993 (before NAFTA). These changes had a direct impact on the border region. With the number of freight cars that made the Piedras Negras-Eagle Pass crossing tripling from 50,000 to 150,000 in the first three years, the twin city challenged Laredo-Nuevo Laredo (which accounted for 60 percent of rail traffic) for first place.

The main turn of events in the early NAFTA period was an increase in intra-industry trade, that is, the exchange of goods within manufacturing sectors and within firms. Such items as electrical machinery, electricity-distribution equipment, telecommunications equipment, office machinery parts, furniture, and automatic data processing machinery topped the list of goods shipped to and from both countries. NAFTA clearly intensified the integration of the two economies rather than distancing them. Although it was tempting to attribute all post-1994 changes to NAFTA, however, post-NAFTA trade clearly followed significant earlier increases that came on the heels of Mexico's entry into GATT in 1986 and the influence of the Salinas years.

As for employment, while union studies documented 96,000 jobs that moved to Mexico between 1980 and 1995, that number was less than the average monthly fluctuation in the size of the U.S. work force. In 1997, *Newsweek* reported that 38,148 jobs were lost at 286 firms as a result of NAFTA but noted that 3 million had been created in the United States in the same period. U.S. unemployment reached a historical low of 4.8 percent, with 2.5 million jobs created in 1996 alone.[24]

The most serious problems under NAFTA were those that had existed long before 1994. Much of the effect of the trade agreement was symbolic: Mexico *appeared* to be a more secure investment site; that is, tying Mexico to the United States *appeared* to lower the risk of Mexican investments. As was revealed during the Mexican economic crisis of 1994–95, however, appearances of stability could be deceiving. Additionally, in this world of new symbolic dynamics, employers could and did threaten to move to Mexico—even if they had no intention of doing so. And labor problems persisted throughout the Mexican border states. Institutionalized sexual harassment was commonplace in the *maquilas*, where male supervisors sometimes exploited their positions to extort sexual favors from female employees, and where pregnant women were sometimes fired.[25] *Maquila* workers found it difficult to form independent labor unions. When they were successful, such efforts were generally greeted by official hostility and usually lasted only a short time.[26] The border environment met with little improvement under NAFTA, at least in the early period. NADBank and BECC—the two agencies set up to address pollution problems along the border—were slow to begin operations: for nearly five years after NAFTA began, not one project financed by NADBank was up and running. For the most part, environmental problems continued unabated.[27]

Looking at specific border-area impacts of NAFTA reveals winners and losers in the agreement. In general, businesses that benefited from freer trade were those that were already competitive, that is, industries that were operating with great efficiency and were active in the global marketplace. The losers were enterprises that were highly protected under Mexico's postwar development model; these operations were either driven out of business or were forced to become competitive.

In terms of trade specifically (ironically, trade was frequently over-looked in discussions of the agreement), it would appear at first glance that the border region achieved what it was after. Border merchants in Mexico had long fought to import goods duty free from the United States for sale in their shops. But national producers and central-government officials frequently argued that special treatment would stifle domestic production. With NAFTA, tensions between producers and consumers were sometimes aggravated by the new rules. For example, in 1995 a supermarket chain in Tijuana began to import milk from a dairy in Yuma, Arizona. Local producers and the only pasteurizing plant in the region immediately complained, saying that the local facility produced enough milk and that the Mexican milk industry would suffer and Mexican jobs would be lost if the U.S. product was sold in Tijuana. Local Baja California officials from the Ministry of Agriculture ordered a ban on milk products from the United States, and U.S. officials protested that the action was a violation of NAFTA. The Mexican federal government eventually intervened to resume U.S. milk sales.

Some observers argued that NAFTA would lead to the demise of *maquila* production; others argued that the whole country would become one giant *maquiladora*. It is true that the trade advantage of the *maquila-doras* ceased under NAFTA. But the comparative advantage of the far north-ern region of Mexico was certain to continue into the foreseeable future. The position of plants close to the U.S. market, their role in coproduction, and their wage rates were all still attractions. Little net effect beyond a name change was likely.

In agriculture inefficient producers on the border were increasingly unable to compete. The basic-grains sector of Mexico is one example. At the end of 1992, Mexican corn cost 240 dollars per ton, while Iowa corn bought at the border went for 110 dollars per ton. Under NAFTA, Mexico gradually increased import quotas and eventually replaced all but residual subsistence production of corn in Mexico. The ten-year phase-in period under NAFTA was a response to social and political realities in Mexico: the years after the 1980s had proved devastating for Mexico's 2.7 million corn producers.

The main impact of the agricultural terms of NAFTA was felt by vegetable growers who catered to the U.S. winter market. NAFTA did not fundamentally change access, which had been expanding rapidly in the 1980s and early 1990s. It did, however, create a more stable environment for investment in export agriculture. Mexican producers on or near the border challenged the market dominance of the U.S. states of California and Florida. Conflicts over tomatoes, avocados, green peppers, oranges, strawberries, grapes, raisins, broccoli, and other crops joined long-standing disagreements over more traditional Mexican exports such as cattle and cotton.

U.S. producers employed various means—sanitary regulations, for example—to stem the flow of inexpensive Mexican crops across the border. Tomatoes emerged as a focal point of dissension. As Mexican growers captured 63 percent of the U.S. winter tomato market in 1995–96, U.S. producers—long threatened by Mexico's seasonal advantage—lodged two formal complaints with the International Trade Commission (ITC), petitioning for relief from competition across the border. In October 1996 Mexican growers relented, agreeing to sell their tomatoes at or above the reference price desired by Florida farmers: ironically, consumers were left holding the bag, forced to pay higher prices that constituted a windfall for producers in both countries.[28] A similar battle was played out with avocado production.

In effect, NAFTA introduced few new factors into the equation of U.S.-Mexican economic relations. Two circumstances in particular combined to ensure this outcome. First, trade between the United States and Mexico had been relatively free before NAFTA was signed in 1994. Mexico had unilaterally lowered its tariffs and opened its economy to U.S. imports after 1985. Notwithstanding the distortions masked by average figures, in 1993 Mexican tarriffs stood at roughly 5 percent and U.S. tariffs stood at twice that amount.[29] Additionally, about 45 percent of Mexican exports to the United States entered duty free under the GSP. Second—and perhaps the most important overlooked context for discussions of free trade in North America—NAFTA did not change the difference in size between the two economies. The U.S. economy towered over its Mexican counterpart: the much ballyhooed "world's biggest and richest market of $6.2 trillion [1994 dollars]" was made up of the United States's 6-trillion-dollar and Mexico's 0.2-trillion-dollar markets. Mexico's GDP was roughly the size of the gross product of Los Angeles County (which had one-tenth Mexico's population); the U.S. trade deficit with Mexico was one-tenth of 1 percent of the U.S. economy. Given this basic asymmetry of proportion, most scholars agreed that NAFTA would affect Mexico much more profoundly than it would affect the United States.

It is important to note also that, as of this writing, NAFTA has not brought free trade—that is, a complete elimination of tariffs and quantitative controls—to North America; instead it provides thousands of pages of trade regulations. And, in addition to the mandated ten-to-fifteen-year phase-ins, there have been successful attempts in both the United States and Mexico to brake the forward motion of the free-trade train. In 1995 and 1996, for example, the Clinton administration delayed the implementation of NAFTA with respect to both the movement of Mexican trucks across the border and the importation of Mexican tomatoes. Between 1996 and 1999 U.S and Mexican truckers were to have the freedom to carry cargo inside the states on the U.S.-Mexican border; in the year 2000 complete cross-border access was to be granted. Citing concerns about the safety of Mexican trucks, the lack of insurance coverage, and the problem of drug trafficking, the U.S government implemented a fourteen-month delay in opening U.S. roads to Mexican truckers beyond a twenty-mile-wide border trade zone; the act was clearly a concession to the Teamsters Union. As election time neared, the Clinton administration also appeased vegetable growers in Florida by pressuring Mexico to stop the shipment of 800 million dollars' worth of low-price tomatoes into the United States. As the White House noted, Florida had twenty-five electoral votes; Mexico had none.

Meanwhile, Mexican government officials also covertly withdrew from some of the NAFTA agreement. In industries such as package delivery, agriculture, and consumer products, nontariff barriers and other unofficial means were employed to limit imports and protect domestic enterprises in manufacturing and services. Mexico established standards that impeded the entry of U.S. grains, citrus fruits, cherries, peaches, and other goods. Senior ministers of the Zedillo government openly discussed protectionist notions such as import substitution, clearly in conflict with a North American free-trade regime. Conflicts over antidumping claims and countervailing duties impositions also loomed. It became apparent that real free trade was not on the region's immediate horizon.

We have seen that myriad bilateral border issues have certain traits in common. The nature of the border—long, porous, unmarked, and unguarded for most of its length—creates complex problems that are particularly difficult to solve. The fact that the border divides two legal systems and two systems of authority makes cumbersome transboundary, collaborative resolution of matters a necessity.

The geographical isolation of the U.S. and Mexican states from the centers of political power—Washington, DC, and Mexico City—complicates the resolution of problems stemming from domestic trends and bilateral relations. Residents of the border region have felt neglected and misunderstood by federal officials and policymakers. In the 1980s, however, the area attracted increasing attention in both national capitals: an Office of Border Affairs was created in the U.S. Department of State, and U.S. congressional groups meet regularly to discuss border issues. In Mexico, El Colegio de la Frontera Norte, founded with government support as a branch of the prestigious Colegio de México, serves as the northern border's graduate-level think tank.

At the same time, since the 1950s, mechanisms for dealing with problems as they arise have been developing with convocations of local authorities. At many points along the boundary local officials have worked out bilateral agreements on such issues as pollution, tourism, transportation, and industrialization. Governors of the ten border states meet regularly, and over time they have addressed substantive matters of common concern to area inhabitants. Such regional political processes may provide the best model for managing the bilateral border relationship into the twenty-first century. Increasingly, U.S. and Mexican leaders at the highest levels have chosen the boundary area as the site for key meetings and acts of state. Both Reagan and Bush chose to meet with their Mexican counterparts at the border to discuss issues of regional, national, and bilateral significance. And in his first official meeting with a foreign leader after his election in 1992, President Bill Clinton joined Salinas in San Antonio, Texas.

A well-known observer of U.S.-Mexican relations has stated that the bilateral relationship is fundamentally structured by three characteristics: "proximity, interpenetration, and asymmetry."[30] These traits are most pronounced at the U.S.-Mexican border, where the two societies meet and intermingle. All three of these qualities as they are expressed in the U.S.-Mexican border region have been transformed over the course of the century. Simple proximity has given way to a complex overlapping and integration; interpenetration has increasingly become interdependence. But disparities in economic might and political power which have great potential to undermine bilateral attempts at problem solving have changed the least.

Despite lingering asymmetries and conflicts over land, water, migration, the environment, and other issues, the society of the border has been remarkable in its adaptation to rapid change and in its capacity to receive migrants seeking new opportunities. Enlightened people on both sides increasingly see their problems as shared challenges and recognize that confronting them will require cooperation across the international boundary and throughout the border region.

NOTES

1. See *Los Angeles Times*, August 29, 1990; February 21, 1991; and September 9, 1995.
2. Bruce Selcraig, "Poisonous Flows the Rio Grande," *Los Angeles Times*, October 25, 1992.
3. A study published by the *American Journal of Epidemiology* found that men who worked with certain chemicals were at least two times more likely than the average male to father an anencephalic child. See Danielle Knight, "Birth Defects Continue in U.S.-Mexico Border Areas" (study produced by Interpress Service [PeaceNet], June 19, 1998).
4. See, for example, Chris Kraul, "A Warmer Climate for Furniture Makers," *Los Angeles Times*, May 14, 1990.
5. See, for example, Lonnie Shavelson, "[Mexican] Border Plants Polluting Salton Sea [in California]," *Times of the Americas*, November 15, 1989.
6. On the environment of the border in general, see Paul Ganster and Hartmut Walter, eds., *Environmental Hazards and Bioresource Management in the United States-Mexico Borderlands* (Los Angeles: UCLA Latin American Center Publications, 1990).
7. Joseph Newman, "Maquiladoras Achieve Only 12 Percent Hazmat Compliance," *EnviroMexico* 9 (November 1996): 1–2.

8. J. Cockroft, *Outlaws in the Promised Land*, p. 107.

9. M. Delal Baer, "Misreading Mexico," *Foreign Policy* (Fall 1997): 146.

10. See William O. Walker, *Drugs in the Western Hemisphere: An Odyssey of Cultures in Conflict* (Wilmington, DE: Scholarly Resources, 1996).

11. Durand and Massey, "Mexican Migration to the United States."

12. David M. Heer, *Undocumented Mexicans in the United States* (New York: Cambridge University Press, 1990); Susan González Baker, *The Cautious Welcome: The Legalization Programs of the Immigration Reform and Control Act* (Santa Monica, CA/Washington, DC: RAND Corporation/Urban Institute, 1990); Charles B. Keely, "Population and Immigration Policy: State and Federal Roles," in *Mexican and Central American Population and U.S. Immigration Policy*, ed. Frank D. Bean, Jurgen Schmandt, and Sidney Weintraub (Austin: University of Texas Press, 1989); Michael C. Lemay, "U.S. Immigration Policy and Politics," in *The Gatekeepers: Comparative Immigration Policy*, ed. Michael C. Lemay (New York: Praeger, 1989); Michael D. Hoefer, "Background of U.S. Immigration Policy Reform," in *U.S. Immigration Policy Reform in the 1980s: A Preliminary Assessment*, ed. Francisco L. Rivera-Batiz, Selig L. Sechzer, and Ira N. Gang (New York: Praeger, 1991); Barry R. Chiswick, "Illegal Immigration and Immigration Control," in Rivera-Batiz, Sechzer, and Gang, *U.S. Immigration Policy Reform*. See also Peter L. Reich, "Jurisprudential Tradition and Undocumented Alien Entitlements," *Georgetown Immigration Law Journal* 6:1 (March 1992): 1–25; and Peter L. Reich, "Public Benefits for Undocumented Aliens: State Law into the Breach Once More," *New Mexico Law Review* 21 (Spring 1991): 219–49. For regional impacts of IRCA in Mexican sending regions, see Jesús Arroyo Alejandre, "Algunos impactos de la Ley de Reforma y Control de Imigración (IRCA) en una región de Jalisco de fuerte emigración hacia Estados Unidos de Norteamérica," in *Estados Unidos y el occidente de México*, ed. Adrían de León Arias (Guadalajara: Universidad de Guadalajara, 1992).

13. See, for example, the study completed for the official Commission on U.S. Immigration Reform: National Research Council, *The New Americans*, pp. 15–19 and passim. See also Mexican Ministry of Foreign Affairs/U.S. Commission on Immigration Reform, *Migration between Mexico and the United States*.

14. See Bean et al., *At the Crossroads;* Agustín Escobar Latapí, Frank D. Bean, and Sidney Weintraub, "The Dynamics of Mexican Migration" (Population Research Center Study, University of Texas, Austin, 1996); and National Research Council, *The New Americans*.

15. See McCarthy and Vernez, *Immigration in a Changing Economy;* "[USC] Study Finds Immigrants' Economic Effect Mixed," *Los Angeles Times,* January 23, 1997; "Immigrants Not Lured by Aid, [Public Policy Institute of California] Study Says," *Los Angeles Times,* January 29, 1997; "Immigrants a Net Economic Plus, [National Research Council] Study Says," *Los Angeles Times,* May 18, 1997; and "U.S.-Mexico Study Sees Exaggeration of Immigration Data," *New York Times,* August 31, 1997.

16. K. Anthony Appiah, "The Multiculturalist Misunderstanding," *New York Review of Books,* October 9, 1997.

17. See Massey, "March of Folly," pp. 22–33.

18. Vernez and McCarthy, *The Costs of Immigration to Taxpayers;* Camarota, "The Labor Market Impact of Immigration."

19. See Massey, "March of Folly"; and National Research Council, *The New Americans,* where old models are critiqued and new ones are proposed.

20. See Sam Fulwood III, "Uncountable Problem at the Border," *Los Angeles Times,* May 17, 1990. For data on border-patrol salaries, ethnic makeup, and other issues, see Sebastian Rotella and Patrick J. McDonnell, "A Seemingly Futile Job Can Breed Abuses by Agents," *Los Angeles Times,* April 23, 1993.

21. See, for example, Marjorie Miller and Patrick McDonnell, "Rise in Violence along Border Brings Call for Action," *Los Angeles Times,* December 9, 1990; Gloria J. Romero and Antonio H. Rodríguez, "A Thousand Points of Xenophobia," *Los Angeles Times,* May 21, 1990; and Rotella and Patrick J. McDonnell, "When Agents Cross over the Borderline," *Los Angeles Times,* April 22, 1993.

22. The best and most balanced studies in a largely polemic literature on free trade and NAFTA are William A. Orme, Jr., *Understanding NAFTA: Mexico, Free Trade, and the New North America* (Austin: University of Texas Press, 1996); and Sidney Weintraub, *NAFTA at Three: A Progress Report* (Washington, DC: Center for Strategic and International Studies [CSIS], 1997).

23. M. Delal Baer and Guy F. Erb, eds., *Strategic Sectors in Mexican-U.S. Free Trade* (Washington, DC: Center for Strategic and International Studies, 1991); Rogelio Ramírez de la O., "A Mexican Vision of North American Economic Integration," in *Continental Accord: North American Economic Integration,* ed. Steven Globerman (Vancouver: Fraser Institute, 1991), pp. 1–30; U.S. Department of Labor, Bureau of Labor Statistics, *Employment and Earnings* 39 (January 1992): 228. For a general overview see Paul Ganster and Eugenio O. Valenciano, eds., *The Mexican-U.S. Border Region and the Free Trade Agreement* (San Diego: Institute for Regional Studies of the Californias, San Diego State University, 1992).

24. Baer, "Misreading Mexico," p. 144.

25. Sam Dillon, "Sex Bias at Border Plants in Mexico Reported by U.S.," *New York Times,* January 13, 1998. See also the story of Irma Leticia López Manzano in Martínez, *Border People,* pp. 186–89.

26. See, for example, "Mexico Overturns Independent Union Victory at Border Factory," *San Francisco Chronicle,* November 15, 1997; Sam Dillon, "Bias Said to Hurt Independent Mexican Unions," *New York Times,* April 30, 1998; David Bacon, "Strike Closes Trailblazing Mexico Plant," *San Francisco Chronicle,* June 2, 1998; and "Justice for Mexican Workers," *San Francisco Chronicle,* June 11, 1998. See also Williams and Passé-Smith, *The Unionization of the Maquiladora Industry.*

27. See Sam Howe Verhovek, "Pollution Puts People in Peril on the Border with Mexico," *New York Times,* July 4, 1998.

28. Stephen Baker and S. Lynne Walker, "Mexico: The Salad Bowl of North America?" *Business Week* (February 25, 1991): 70–71; Bruce F. Johnston et al., eds., *U.S.-Mexican Relations: Agriculture and Rural Development* (Stanford: Stanford University Press, 1987); Armand B. Peschard-Sverdrup, "The U.S.-Mexico Fresh Winter Tomato Trade Dispute: The Broader Implications," *CSIS Policy Paper on the Americas* 7:4 (September 1996).

29. Many goods were not included in the General System of Preferences (GSP), and some high tariffs (some seasonal—tomatoes, for example) were hidden by average figures. See Orme, *Understanding NAFTA,* p. 71.

30. Abraham Lowenthal, *Partners in Conflict: The United States and Latin America* (Baltimore: Johns Hopkins University Press, 1987), p. 77.

SUGGESTED
READINGS

THE BORDERLANDS TO 1910

Benjamin, Thomas, and William McNellie, eds. *Other Mexicos: Essays on Regional History, 1876–1911*. Albuquerque: University of New Mexico Press, 1984.

Brear, Holly. *Inherit the Alamo: Myth and Ritual at an American Shrine*. Austin: University of Texas Press, 1995.

French, William E. *A Peaceful And Working People*. Albuquerque: University of New Mexico Press, 1997.

Moisés, Rosalio, J. H. Kelley, and W. C. Holden. *The Tall Candle: The Personal Chronicle of a Yaqui Indian*. Lincoln: University of Nebraska Press, 1971.

Montejano, David. *Anglos and Mexicans in the Making of Texas, 1836–1986*. Austin: University of Texas Press, 1987.

Ruíz, Ramón Eduardo. *The People of Sonora and Yankee Capitalists*. Tucson: University of Arizona Press, 1988.

Spicer, Edward H. *Cycles of Conquest: The Indians of the Southwest, 1533–1960*. Tucson: University of Arizona Press, 1962.

Voss, Stuart F. *On the Periphery of Nineteenth-Century Mexico: Sonora and Sinaloa, 1810–1877*. Tucson: University of Arizona Press, 1982.

Wasserman, Mark. *Capitalists, Caciques, and Revolution: Chihuahua, Mexico, 1854–1911*. Chapel Hill: University of North Carolina Press, 1984.

Weber, David J. *The Mexican Frontier, 1821–1846: The American Southwest under Mexico.* Albuquerque: University of New Mexico Press, 1982.

———. *Myth and the History of the Hispanic Southwest.* Albuquerque: University of New Mexico Press, 1988.

———. *The Spanish Frontier in North America.* New Haven: Yale University Press, 1992.

THE REVOLUTION, 1910-1929

Benjamin, Thomas, and Mark Wasserman, eds. *Provinces of the Revolution: Regional Mexican History.* Albuquerque: University of New Mexico Press, 1990.

Cardoso, Lawrence. *Mexican Emigration to the United States, 1877–1931.* Tucson: University of Arizona Press, 1980.

Coerver, Don, and Linda B. Hall. *Revolution on the Border: The United States and Mexico, 1910–1920.* Albuquerque: University of New Mexico Press, 1988.

Cumberland, Charles. "The Sonora Chinese and the Mexican Revolution," *Hispanic American Historical Review* 40 (1960): 191–211.

Deutsch, Sarah. *No Separate Refuge: Culture, Class, and Gender on an Anglo-Hispanic Frontier, 1880–1940.* New York: Oxford University Press, 1987.

Gamio, Manuel. *The Mexican Immigrant: His Life Story.* Chicago: University of Chicago Press, 1931.

Garcia, Juan. *Mexicans in the Midwest, 1900–1932.* Tucson: University of Arizona Press, 1996.

Harris, Charles H., and Louis R. Sadler. *The Border and the Revolution: Clandestine Activities, 1910–1920.* Las Cruces: Center for Latin American Studies/Joint Border Research Institute, New Mexico State University, 1988.

Justice, Glenn. *Revolution on the Rio Grande: Mexican Raids and Army Pursuits, 1916–1919.* El Paso: Western Press, 1992.

Katz, Friedrich. "Pancho Villa: Reform Governor of Chihuahua." In *Essays on the Mexican Revolution: Revisionist Views of the Leaders.* Edited by William H. Beezley. Austin: University of Texas Press, 1979.

Raat, Dirk W. *Revoltosos: Mexico's Rebels in the United States, 1903–1923.* College Station: Texas A&M University Press, 1981.

Sandos, James A. *Rebellion in the Borderlands: Anarchism and the Plan of San Diego, 1904–1923.* Norman: University of Oklahoma Press, 1992.

Zamora, Emilio. *The World of the Mexican Worker in Texas.* College Station: Texas A&M University Press, 1993.

BORDER TOWNS

Arreola, Daniel D., and James R. Curtis. *The Mexican Border Cities.* Tucson: University of Arizona Press, 1993.

Camarrillo, Albert. *Chicanos in a Changing Society: Santa Barbara and Southern California, 1848–1930.* Cambridge: Harvard University Press, 1996.

Cardoso, Lawrence A. *Mexican Emigration to the United States, 1897–1931.* Tucson: University of Arizona Press, 1980.

D'Antonio, William, and William Form. *Influentials in Two Border Cities.* Notre Dame: University of Notre Dame Press, 1965.

Gamboa, Erasmo. *Mexican Labor and World War II: Braceros in the Pacific Northwest, 1942–1947.* Austin: University of Texas Press, 1990.

García, Mario T. *Desert Immigrants: The Mexicans of El Paso, 1880–1920.* New Haven: Yale University Press, 1981.

Hinojosa, Gilberto Miguel. *A Borderlands Town in Transition: Laredo, 1755–1870.* College Station: Texas A&M University Press, 1983.

Kearney, Milo, and Anthony Knopp. *Boom and Bust: The Historical Cycles of Matamoros and Brownsville.* Austin, TX: Eakin Press, 1991.

Klein, Alan M. *Baseball at the Border: A Tale of Two Laredos.* Princeton: Princeton University Press, 1997.

León, Arnoldo de. *The Tejano Community, 1836–1900.* Dallas: Southern Methodist University Press, 1997.

Lister, Florence C., and Robert H. Lister *Chihuahua: Storehouse of Storms.* Albuquerque: University of New Mexico Press, 1966.

Martinez, Oscar J. *Border Boom Town: Ciudad Juárez since 1848.* Austin: University of Texas Press, 1978.

Mélendez-Ocasio, Marcel "Mexican Urban History: The Case of Tampico, Tamaulipas, 1876–1924." Ph.D. diss., Michigan State University, 1988.

Price, John A. *Tijuana: Urbanization in a Border Culture.* Notre Dame: University of Notre Dame Press, 1973.

Romo, Ricardo. *East Los Angeles: History of a Barrio.* Austin: University of Texas Press, 1983.

Saragoza, Alex. *The Monterrey Elite and the Mexican State, 1880–1940.* Austin: University of Texas Press, 1988.

Sheridan, Thomas E. *Los Tucsoneses: The Mexican Community in Tucson, 1854–1941.* Tucson: University of Arizona Press, 1986.

Timmons, Wilbert H. *El Paso: A Borderlands History.* El Paso: University of Texas Press, 1990.

Young, Gay, ed. *The Social Ecology and Economic Development of Ciudad Juárez.* Boulder: Westview Press, 1986.

MIGRATION

Alvarez, Robert R. *Familia: Migration and Adaptation in Baja and Alta California, 1800–1975.* Berkeley: University of California Press, 1987.

Bean, Frank D., Rodolfo O. de la Garza, Bryan R. Roberts, and Sidney Weintraub. *At the Crossroads: Mexican and U.S. Immigration Policy.* New York: Rowman and Littlefield, 1997.

Camarota, Steven A. "The Labor Market Impact of Immigration: A Review of Recent Studies," *Center for Immigration Studies Backgrounder,* no. 1–98 (May 1998).

Cardoso, Lawrence A. *Mexican Emigration to the United States, 1877–1931.* Tucson: University of Arizona Press, 1980.

Chavez, Leo R. *Shadowed Lives: Undocumented Immigrants in American Society.* Fort Worth: Harcourt Brace College Publishers, 1998.

Durand, Jorge, and Douglas S. Massey. "Mexican Migration to the United States: A Critical Review," *Latin American Research Review* 27: 2 (1992): 3–42.

Guerin-Gonzales, Camille. *Mexican Workers and American Dreams: Immigration, Repatriation, and California Farm Labor, 1900–1939.* New Brunswick, NJ: Rutgers University Press, 1994.

Gutiérrez, David G. *Between Two Worlds: Mexican Immigrants in the United States.* Wilmington, DE: Scholarly Resources, 1996.

Jones, Richard C. *Ambivalent Journey: U.S. Migration and Economic Mobility in North-Central Mexico.* Tucson: University of Arizona Press, 1995.

Lozano Ascencio, Fernando. *Bringing It Back Home: Remittances to Mexico from Migrant Workers.* La Jolla: Center for U.S.-Mexican Studies, UCSD, 1993.

Massey, Douglas S. "March of Folly: U.S. Immigration Policy after NAFTA," *American Prospect* 37 (March–April 1998): 22–33.

———. *Return to Aztlán: The Social Process of International Migration from Western Mexico.* Berkeley: University of California Press, 1987.

McCarthy, Kevin F., and Georges Vernez. *Immigration in a Changing Economy: California's Experience.* Santa Monica: RAND Corporation, 1997.

Mexican Ministry of Foreign Affairs/U.S. Commission on Immigration Reform. *Migration between Mexico and the United States: Binational Study/Estudio Binacional Mexico-Estados Unidos sobre Migración.* Mexico City/Washington, DC: Mexican Ministry of Foreign Affairs/U.S. Commission on Immigration Reform, 1998.

National Research Council. *The New Americans: Economic, Demographic, and Fiscal Effects of Immigration.* Edited by J. P. Smith and B. Edmonton. Washington, DC: National Academy Press, 1997.

Vernez, Georges, and Kevin F. McCarthy. *The Costs of Immigration to Taxpayers: Analytical and Policy Issues.* Santa Monica: RAND Corporation, 1997.

CONTEMPORARY ISSUES

Balderrama, Francisco E., and Raymond Rodríguez. *Decade of Betrayal: Mexican Repatriation in the 1930s.* Albuquerque: University of New Mexico Press, 1995.

Hansen, Niles. *The Border Economy: Regional Development in the Southwest.* Austin: University of Texas Press, 1981.

Hart, John Mason. *Border Crossings: Mexican and Mexican-American Workers.* Wilmington, DE: Scholarly Resources, 1998.

Herzog, Lawrence. *Where North Meets South: Cities, Space, and Politics on the U.S.-Mexico Border.* Austin: Center for Mexican American Studies, University of Texas, 1990.

Heyman, Josiah McC. *Life and Labor on the Border: Working People of Northeastern Sonora, 1889–1986.* Tucson: University of Arizona Press, 1991.

Kingsolver, Barbara. *Holding the Line: Women in the Great Arizona Mine Strike of 1983.* New York: ILR Press, 1996.

Lowenthal, Abraham, and Katrina Burgess. *The California-Mexico Connection.* Stanford: Stanford University Press, 1993.

Machado, Manuel A. *The North Mexican Cattle Industry, 1910–1975: Ideology, Conflict, and Change.* College Station: Texas A&M University Press, 1981.

Maril, Robert Lee. *Living on the Edge of America: At Home on the Texas-Mexico Border.* College Station: Texas A&M University Press, 1992.

Martínez, Oscar J. *Border People: Life and Society in the U.S.-Mexico Borderlands.* Tucson: University of Arizona Press, 1994.

———. *Troublesome Border.* Tucson: University of Arizona Press, 1988.

———, ed. *U.S.-Mexico Borderlands: Historical and Contemporary Perspectives.* Wilmington, DE: Scholarly Resources, 1996.

Ross, Stanley R., ed. *Views Across the Border: The United States and Mexico.* Albuquerque: University of New Mexico Press, 1978.

Ruíz, Vicki L., and Susan Tiano, eds. *Women on the U.S.-Mexico Border: Responses to Change.* Boston: Allen and Unwin, 1987.

Simon, Joel. *Endangered Mexico: An Environment on the Edge.* San Francisco: Sierra Club Books, 1997.

Stoddard, Ellwyn. *Trends and Patterns of Poverty Along the U.S.-Mexico Border.* Las Cruces: Joint Border Research Institute, New Mexico State University, 1987.

Vargas, Zaragosa. "Armies in the Fields and Factories: The Mexican Working Classes in the Midwest in the 1920s," *Mexican Studies/Estudios Mexicanos* 7:1 (Winter 1991): 47–71.

MAQUILADORAS

Fatemi, Khosrow, ed. *The Maquiladora Industry: Economic Solution or Problem?* New York: Praeger, 1990.

Fernández-Kelly, María Patricia. *For We Are Sold, I and My People: Women and Industry in Mexico's Frontier.* Albany: State University of New York Press, 1983.

Sklair, Leslie. *Assembling for Development: The Maquila Industry in Mexico and the United States.* San Diego: Center for U.S.-Mexican Studies, University of California, 1989.

Stoddard, Ellwyn R. *Maquila: Assembly Plants in Northern Mexico.* El Paso: Texas Western Press, 1987.

Williams, Edward J., and John T. Passé-Smith. *The Unionization of the Maquiladora Industry: The Tamaulipan Case in National Context.* San Diego: Institute for Regional Studies of the Californias, San Diego State University, 1992.

Wilson, Patricia A. *Exports and Local Development: Mexico's New Maquiladoras.* Austin: University of Texas Press, 1992.

REFERENCE

Lorey, David, ed. *United States-Mexico Border Statistics since 1900.* Los Angeles: UCLA Latin American Center Publications, 1990.

———, ed. *United States-Mexico Border Statistics since 1900: 1990 Update.* Los Angeles: UCLA Latin American Center Publications, 1993.

Ochoa, Enrique C. "Constructing *Fronteras*: Teaching the History of the U.S.-Mexico Borderlands in the Age of Proposition 187 and Free Trade," *Radical History Review* 70 (1998): 116–28.

INDEX

Adams-Onís Treaty (1819), 26, 28
Aerospace industry, 84
African Americans: in frontier society, 21, 26; in labor force, 54; Plan de San Diego and, 68
Agrarian reform, 80–81
Agricultural production, 19, 43–44, 48, 62, 85, 86–88, 95–98; boom and bust, 44; disrupted by Revolution, 43; expanded by railroads, 38; impact of NAFTA on, 176; mechanized, 86–87; scientific farming, 87; statistics, 95–98; surge in Southwest, 48. *See also* Braceros and Bracero Program
Agua Caliente casino, 46–47
Aguascalientes, 44
Aguayo, Marques de, 18, 27
Albuquerque: as railroad center, 48; climate promoted, 74
All-American Canal, 79, 84
Allende, Encarnación, 138–39
Alonso, María Conchita, 145

Alta California, 25
Alurista, 146
Alvarez de Pineda, Alonso, 18
American Smelting and Refining Company (ASARCO), 38, 48
Apache Indians, 17, 22, 26, 56, 58, 64
Arizona, 8, 42, 49, 59, 79–80, 102
Arizona Canal, 43
Arkansas River, 27
Armijo, Manuel, 27
Asians: in labor force, 54
Atchison, Topeka, and Santa Fe Railroad, 36
Avila, Jesús, 123
Austin, Moses, 26
Austin, Stephen, 26

Baja California, 8, 55, 133–34; statehood, 120
Banditry, 61, 67
Bank of America, 85
Banks and banking, 61, 78, 113, 160, 170

Barrio, Francisco, 133
Béjar, 26
Beltrán Hernández, Irene, 146
Bisbee, 42, 54
Boeing Corp., 83
Border Aid Program, 103
Border crossings, 3, 70, 122–23
Border Environmental Cooperation
    Commission (BECC), 160, 174
Border Incident (movie), 145
Border Industrialization Program (BIP),
    104–5
Border Patrol (U.S.), 167–68
Boulder Dam, 79
Bowman, Wirt G., 46
Braceros and Bracero Program, 89–90, 91,
    101, 120, 121–22, 124, 163; abuses,
    122–23
Brazos, 26
Bronson, Charles, 145
Brownsville, 30, 67, 125
Bush, George, 160, 178

Cabeza de Vaca, Alvar Núñez, 18
Calexico, 3
California, 8, 28, 31, 85, 90, 119, 134,
    136–37, 158–59; agricultural boom,
    43–44; as oil producer, 42; U.S. offer
    to buy, 29; wartime boom, 83–84
California Institute of Technology, 84
Californios, 55
Calles, Plutarco Elías, 66, 81
Camargo, 30
Canadian River, 27
Cananea, 55, 60, 108
Cananea Consolidated Copper Company,
    59
Capone, Al, 47
Cárdenas, Lázaro, 80, 95
Cárdenas, Margarita Cota, 146
Carranza, Venustiano, 63, 65, 66, 69, 81,
    133
Casinos, 46
Central Railroad, 36, 54
Central Valley, 44
Chamizal dispute, 154–55
Chávez, César, 135
Chihuahua, 8, 55, 64–65, 102, 133;
    Porfirian progress in, 57–63; rail link
    to U.S., 58

Chinese: in labor force, 54, 59–60
Cíbola, 18
Ciudad Victoria, 55
Civilian Conservation Corps, 79
Civilian Works Administration, 79
Clifton, 54
Clinton, Bill, 177, 179
Coahuila, 8, 19, 37, 55, 102, 137–39;
    Texans joined to, 24
Cochise, 56
Colonial period, 17–23
Colonias, 5, 130, 158
Colorado River: aqueduct, 84; disputes
    over flow, 155–56
Colorado River Land Company, 80–81
Columbus: Villa's attack on, 66
Comanche Indians, 22, 26
Commerce: foreign, 24–25
Confederación de Trabajadores de
    México, 91
Conover, Ted, 122
Constitution of 1824 (Mexico), 24
Consumer goods: imported for resale,
    113
Convicts: as settlers, 28
Copper, 42–43, 48, 89
Coronado, Francisco Vásquez de, 18
Corral, Ramón, 62
Corridos, 144
Cost of living, 131
Cotton, 43, 87
Creel, Enrique, 58, 59
Creel family, 56
Creelman, James, 62
Crofton, James N., 46
Crosby, Bing, 47
Cruise, Tom, 145
Culture: and border society, 5, 16,
    139–47

Defense expenditures, 82–87, 94–95,
    113–14
Dehesa, Teodoro, 62–63
Del Rio, 30
Díaz, Porfirio, 35–36, 40, 55, 56–63,
    141; free trade and, 49–50. *See also*
    "Order and Progress"
Disease: causes of death, 132; effect on
    native population, 21, 25; and popula-
    tion growth, 130

Doheny, Edward L., 39
Domestic animals, 22
Douglas, 30, 42, 54
Douglas Aircraft Corp., 81
Drugs and drug trafficking, 5, 6, 161–62, 177
Durango, 8
Durante, Jimmy, 47

Eagle Pass, 30, 173
Echeverría, Luis, 113
Economy: described on border region, 40–41
Education: of migrants, 164
Ejidos, 80–81, 87, 98
El Aguila. *See* Mexican Eagle Company
El Continental, 130
El Fronterizo, 130–31
El Paso, 3, 30, 44, 48–49, 74–75, 78, 81, 104, 129, 136, 154, 158; climate promoted, 74; effect of railroad on, 37, 48–49; as mining center, 42–43, 48; Prohibition and, 46
El Paso Electric Company, 46
El Paso Herald Post, 81
Electronics industry, 84
Elephant Butte Dam, 43
Employment rates, 48, 174
Environment, 5, 158–61, 174
Environmental Protection Agency (EPA), 161
Espaldas mojadas (movie), 145
European Americans: in labor force, 54
Exploration, 18–19

Fairbanks, Douglas, 47
Farm Security Administration (FSA), 89–90
Federal Relief Emergency Administration, 79
Florida, 177
Food processing, 43–44
Foreign investment, 36, 38, 39–40, 50, 105–6, 108, 174
Fort Bliss, 85, 88–89
Fort Duncan, 30
Fort Ord, 85
Franciscans, 20
Free trade, 32–33, 49–50, 81–82, 113, 160. *See also* Trade

Fronterizos, 50, 82, 139
Frontier: population described, 20–21, 23; U.S. settlers encouraged, 28
Fundidora Monterrey, 39

Gable, Clark, 47
Gadsden Purchase (1853), 6, 29
Galarza, Ernesto, 146
Galindo, Alejandro, 145
General Agreement on Tariffs and Trade (GATT), 169, 173
General Dynamics Corp., 94
Geographical factors, 15–16
Geronimo, 56
Gold, 38–39
Gold rush (California), 31, 32, 39
Gomes, Estevão de, 18
Gran Chichimeca, 18, 22
Great Depression, 40, 44, 71, 74, 78–82
Gross domestic product, 86, 95–97, 171, 177
Gross national product, 82
Guadalupe, 30
Guanajuato, 18
Guaymas, 55
Guerrero, 30
Guggenheim, Daniel, 38
Gwin Land Act (1851), 31

Harlow, Jean, 47
Health care, 131, 132
Hearst, William Randolph, 39
Hermosillo, 55
High-tech industry, 82–83, 91, 94–95, 100–101
HIV infection, 130, 162
Hoover Dam, 79, 84
Housing, 130–32
Hughes Aircraft Corp., 94
Hyundai Corp., 110

Immigration acts (U.S.), 70–71, 73, 163
Immigration and Nationality Act, 163
Immigration and Naturalization Service (INS), 121, 167
Immigration Reform and Control Act (IRCA), 163–64
Imperial Dam, 43
Imperial Valley, 38, 84
Income: per capita, 85

Independence (Mexico), 23–24
Independence (Texas), 28
Indian dialects, 16–17
Indian (indigenous) peoples, 16–18, 21, 22, 25, 55–56; affected by disease, 21; European influences on, 22. *See also by group*
Industrialization, 85–86, 104–13
Inflation, 113
International Boundary and Water Commission, 155–56
International Boundary Commission, 155
International Trade Commission (ITC), 176
Irrigation projects, 43, 47–48, 67, 80, 81, 86, 87–88; statistics, 88
Islas, Arturo, 146

Jalisco, 8
Japanese: Plan de San Diego and, 68
Jefes políticos, 57
Jesuits, 20
Juárez (Ciudad Juárez), 3, 47, 50, 72, 74–75, 78, 89, 104, 125, 130–31, 154, 158; described, 43–44; Prohibition and, 46
Juntas de beneficiencia, 72

Kahlo, Frida, 145
Kaiser Corp., 83
Keaton, Buster, 47
Korean War, 90, 122

La Mesilla, 30
La Paz, 55
Labor, 53–54, 59–60, 70, 89–90, 91, 101–2, 109–10, 171; in agriculture, 54, 71; in mining, 54; on railroads, 59, 71
Labor Department (U.S.): and *maquiladoras,* 110
Land and landholding, 27; redistribution, 80–81; title disputes, 31–32
Laredo, 30, 173
Life expectancy, 131
Linares, 55
Literature, 146
Livestock raising, 39, 41
Lockheed Corp., 81, 94
Long, Baron, 46

Long, Shelley, 145
López, Luis, 123
Los Angeles, 54, 124, 136; as largest border city, 75
Los Lobos, 144
Louisiana Purchase (1803), 6, 26

Madero, Evaristo, 38
Madero, Francisco I., 61, 62–63, 66, 133; *Presidential Succession,* 61
Madrid, Miguel de la, 169
Mangas Coloradas, 56
Manifest Destiny: promoted, 28
Mann, Arthur, 145
Manufacturing, 41, 42, 84; expansion, 39; statistics, 98–101
Maquilas and *maquiladoras,* 2, 5, 8–9, 105–13, 123, 140, 159, 174, 175; statistics, 108, 109
Martínez, Oscar, 122; *Border People,* 127–28, 135
Marx brothers, 47
Matamoros, 30, 67, 125
Mazatlán, 55
McAllen, 30, 68
McDonnell-Douglas Corp., 94
Mendez, Miguel, 146
Mexicali, 3, 95
Mexican Eagle Company (El Aguila), 39
Mexican Miracle (1950s–1960s), 86, 87
Mexican Petroleum Company, 39
Mexico City: control of northern states, 57
Mier, 30
Migrants and migration, 54, 55, 67–68, 84–85, 89–90, 119, 120–22, 123, 124, 162–69, 171–72; impact of Revolution on, 69–73; sending communities, 137–39; statistics, 101–2
Military: wartime economy and, 84–85, 94
Mining, 18, 38–39, 42–43, 85, 102; unemployment in, 61–62. *See also* Copper; Gold; Silver mining
Missions, 21; as key to settlement, 20, 125; secularization, 22
Monterrey (Nuevo León), 86, 91, 98, 100, 111, 124–25; as fastest-growing city, 55; as industrial center, 39
Monterrey Tech, 86

Morales, Alejandro, 146
Morenci, 42
Motorola Corp., 94
Movies (films), 145–46, 170
Mulegé, 55
Music: popular, 144
Muzquiz, 55

Nacogdoches, 26
NAFINSA, 103
Navajo Indians, 17
Navojoa, 55
New Deal, 77, 79
New Mexico, 8, 31, 79–80
Newsweek, 174
Nicholson, Jack, 145
Nightclubs and bars: in border towns, 46–47
Nogales, 30
Nolte, Nick, 145
North American Development Bank (NADBank), 160–61, 174
North American Free Trade Agreement (NAFTA), 5, 110–11, 160, 169–77; statistics, 173
Nueva Vizcaya, 18
Nuevo Laredo, 30, 173; effect of railroad on, 37
Nuevo León, 8, 55
Nuevo México, 27
Nuñez Cabeza de Vaca, Alvar, 18

Obregón, Alvaro, 66, 81, 133
Operation Gatekeeper, 168
Operation Hold the Line, 168
Operation Wetback, 121–22
"Order and Progress" (under President Díaz), 36, 56, 57, 60–61
Oregon Territory, 6
Otis, Harrison Gray, 39

Pachuca, 18
Padilla, Manuel, 122
Parral, 18
Partido de Acción Nacional (PAN), 133
Partido Nacional Revolucionario, 41
Partido Revolucionario Institucional (PRI), 133
Paz, Octavio, 117
Pearson, Whitman, 39

Pecos River, 27
Perot, Ross, 5
Pershing, General John J., 66
Petroleum, 39, 41–42; oil prices, 50, 113, 169
Phelps Dodge Corp., 48
Piedras Negras, 30, 55, 173
Plan de San Diego, 68–69
Pollution, 174
Ponce de León, Juan, 18
Population rates, 16, 67–68, 73–74, 78, 87, 118–19, 125
Portes Gil, Emilio, 66
Poverty 5, 70, 131–33, 136
Powell, Dick, 47
Presidio (San Francisco), 85
Presidios: as key to settlement, 20, 23–24, 125
Programa Nacional Fronterizo (PRONAF), 103–4, 146–47
Prohibition: effect on border economy, 45–48, 81–82, 89, 161
Prostitution: in border towns, 5, 46

Quejo, Pedro de, 18

Railroads, 47, 49, 54–55, 59, 141; Chihuahua-U.S. link, 58; construction and development, 36–38, 40; destruction during Revolution, 43; Mexicanized by Díaz, 40; as transportation for migrants, 69; wartime, 89
Ramos, Basilio, 68
Rancherías, 17
Reagan, Ronald, 103, 178
Reclamation Act (1902), 43
Reconstruction Finance Agency, 79
Recruitment: of settlers, 30
Refugio, 30
Remittances: from migrant workers, 139
Repatriation and repatriados, 30, 71–72
Revolution of 1910 (Mexico), 41–43, 62–66, 70, 74; and Díaz's "Order and Progress," 56–63; as stimulus to growth, 69
Reynosa, 30
Río Bravo/Rio Grande River, 43, 79; changes in course, 154–55; disputes over flow, 157
Rio Grande City, 30

Roads, 88
Rockwell International Corp., 94
Rodrigues Cabrilho, João, 18
Rodríguez, Abelardo, 66
Rondstadt, Linda, 144
Roosevelt, Franklin D., 77, 83
Roosevelt Dam, 43
Ruffo, Ernesto, 133

Sabinas, 55
Salinas: effect of railroad on, 37
Salinas de Gortari, Carlos, 160, 169, 173, 179
Salt River Valley, 38
Saltillo, 55
Salton Sea, 158
San Antonio, 54, 98, 100, 138
San Diego, 125, 127, 160
San Joaquin Valley, 54
San Luis Potosí, 18
Sánchez Navarro family, 27
Santa Anna, Antonio López de, 24, 29
Santo Tomás, 30
Scott, Winfield, 29
Selena, 144
Sierra Madre, 15–16
Silicon Valley, 94–95, 100–101
Silver mining, 18–19, 39
Sinaloa, 8, 20
Slavery: abolished in Mexico, 28
Smuggling, 33, 41, 67
Sonora, 8, 37–38, 47, 102, 142; U.S. investment in, 40
Sonora Land and Cattle Company, 40
Soto, Hernando de, 18
Southern Pacific Railroad, 36, 49, 54
Southwestern Railroad, 49
Soviet Union: effect of collapse of, 113–14
Spaniards: resistance to, 23
Sperry Corp., 94
Stanford University, 84
Steel production, 39

Tamaulipas, 8, 102
Tampico, 55
Tariffs, 169; waived in free-trade area, 49–50, 82. See also General Agreement on Tariffs and Trade
Taxes, 28
Tejanos, 31, 55

Terrazas, Luis, 58, 59, 64
Terrazas family, 56, 61
Texas, 26–27, 31, 67–69, 113, 134, 170; annexed by U.S., 29; independence recognized, 28; as oil producer, 42; U.S. offer to buy, 28
Texas Instruments Corp., 94
Texas Rangers, 69
Tijuana, 2, 30, 72, 75, 78, 81, 95, 102, 125, 127, 160; Prohibition and, 46–47
Tomóchic, 60
Torréon Metallurgical Company, 38
Tourism and tourists, 5, 45, 81, 88, 102–3, 170; decline during Depression, 78
Trade, 24–25, 36, 38, 41, 89, 173, 175, 177; free zones, 32–33, 49–50. See also Free Trade; General Agreement on Tariffs and Trade
Travis Air Force Base, 85
Treaty of Guadalupe Hidalgo (1848), 29, 31, 32, 154
Tucson: climate promoted, 49, 74, 79; as railroad center, 48, 49
Twin cities (sister cities), 3, 30, 44–45, 67; described, 125–30; statistics, 126; Ciudad Juárez-El Paso, 67, 75, 125–26; Laredo-Nuevo Laredo, 173; Matamoros-Brownsville, 67, 125; Piedras Negras-Eagle Pass, 173; Tijuana-San Diego, 125, 127, 160

Unemployment, 164, 174; in mining, 61–62; in oil industry, 113; statistics, 114
Union Pacific Railroad, 36
Universidad Autónoma de Nuevo León, 86
University of California, 84
Urbanization, 74–75; statistics, 124–25
Urbina, Tomás, 65
U.S.-Mexican relations, 154–79
U.S.-Mexican War (1846–48), 23, 29

Villa, Pancho, 61, 63–66, 80
Villarreal, José, 146
Volstead Act (1919), 45

Wages, 171
War Food Administration, 90

War of the Gran Chichimeca, 22
Water issues, 154–58. *See also* Irrigation
 projects
Weissmuller, Johnny, 47
West Coast: French and English interest
 in, 28
Westinghouse Corp., 83
Wilson, Woodrow, 71
Works Progress Administration, 79
World Bank, 157–58

World War I, 42, 43, 69
World War II: as era of growth, 82–87,
 119

Yaqui Indians, 55–56, 80
Yucatán peninsula, 8, 140

Zacatecas, 18, 44, 137–39
Zapata, Emiliano, 63
Zedillo, Ernesto, 178

Latin American Silhouettes
Studies in History and Culture

William H. Beezley and
Judith Ewell
Editors

Volumes Published

Silvia Marina Arrom and Servando Ortoll, eds., *Riots in the Cities: Popular Politics and the Urban Poor in Latin America, 1765–1910* (1996). Cloth ISBN 0-8420-2580-4   Paper ISBN 0-8420-2581-2

Roderic Ai Camp, ed., *Polling for Democracy: Public Opinion and Political Liberalization in Mexico* (1996). ISBN 0-8420-2583-9

Brian Loveman and Thomas M. Davies, Jr., eds., *The Politics of Antipolitics: The Military in Latin America*, 3d ed., revised and updated (1996). Cloth ISBN 0-8420-2609-6   Paper ISBN 0-8420-2611-8

Joseph S. Tulchin, Andrés Serbín, and Rafael Hernández, eds., *Cuba and the Caribbean: Regional Issues and Trends in the Post-Cold War Era* (1997). ISBN 0-8420-2652-5

Thomas W. Walker, ed., *Nicaragua without Illusions: Regime Transition and Structural Adjustment in the 1990s* (1997). Cloth ISBN 0-8420-2578-2   Paper ISBN 0-8420-2579-0

Dianne Walta Hart, *Undocumented in L.A.: An Immigrant's Story* (1997). Cloth ISBN 0-8420-2648-7   Paper ISBN 0-8420-2649-5

Jaime E. Rodríguez O. and Kathryn Vincent, eds., *Myths, Misdeeds, and Misunderstandings: The Roots of Conflict in U.S.-Mexican Relations* (1997). ISBN 0-8420-2662-2

Jaime E. Rodríguez O. and Kathryn Vincent, eds., *Common Border, Uncommon Paths: Race, Culture, and National Identity in U.S.-Mexican Relations* (1997). ISBN 0-8420-2673-8

William H. Beezley and Judith Ewell, eds., *The Human Tradition in Modern Latin America* (1997). Cloth ISBN 0-8420-2612-6   Paper ISBN 0-8420-2613-4

Donald F. Stevens, ed., *Based on a True Story: Latin American History at the Movies* (1997). Cloth ISBN 0-8420-2582-0   Paper ISBN 0-8420-2781-5

Jaime E. Rodríguez O., ed., *The Origins of Mexican National Politics, 1808–1847* (1997). Paper ISBN 0-8420-2723-8

Che Guevara, *Guerrilla Warfare*, with revised and updated introduction and case studies by Brian Loveman and Thomas M. Davies, Jr., 3d ed. (1997). Cloth ISBN 0-8420-2677-0   Paper ISBN 0-8420-2678-9

Adrian A. Bantjes, *As If Jesus Walked on Earth: Cardenismo, Sonora, and the Mexican Revolution* (1998). ISBN 0-8420-2653-3

Henry A. Dietz and Gil Shidlo, eds., *Urban Elections in Democratic Latin America* (1998). Cloth ISBN 0-8420-2627-4   Paper ISBN 0-8420-2628-2

A. Kim Clark, *The Redemptive Work: Railway and Nation in Ecuador, 1895–1930* (1998). ISBN 0-8420-2674-6

Joseph S. Tulchin, ed., with Allison M. Garland, *Argentina: The Challenges of Modernization* (1998). ISBN 0-8420-2721-1

Louis A. Pérez, Jr., ed., *Impressions of Cuba in the Nineteenth Century: The Travel Diary of Joseph J. Dimock* (1998). Cloth ISBN 0-8420-2657-6   Paper ISBN 0-8420-2658-4

June E. Hahner, ed., *Women through Women's Eyes: Latin American Women in Nineteenth-Century Travel Accounts* (1998). Cloth ISBN 0-8420-2633-9   Paper ISBN 0-8420-2634-7

James P. Brennan, ed., *Peronism and Argentina* (1998). ISBN 0-8420-2706-8

John Mason Hart, ed., *Border Crossings: Mexican and Mexican-American Workers* (1998). Cloth ISBN 0-8420-2716-5   Paper ISBN 0-8420-2717-3

Brian Loveman, *For* la Patria: *Politics and the Armed Forces in Latin America* (1999). Cloth ISBN 0-8420-2772-6 Paper ISBN 0-8420-2773-4

Guy P. C. Thomson, with David G. LaFrance, *Patriotism, Politics, and Popular Liberalism in Nineteenth-Century Mexico: Juan Francisco Lucas and the Puebla Sierra* (1999). ISBN 0-8420-2683-5

Robert Woodmansee Herr, in collaboration with Richard Herr, *An American Family in the Mexican Revolution* (1999). ISBN 0-8420-2724-6

Juan Pedro Viqueira Albán, trans. Sonya Lipsett-Rivera and Sergio Rivera Ayala, *Propriety and Permissiveness in Bourbon Mexico* (1999). Cloth ISBN 0-8420-2466-2 Paper ISBN 0-8420-2467-0

Stephen R. Niblo, *Mexico in the 1940s: Modernity, Politics, and Corruption* (1999). ISBN 0-8420-2794-7

David E. Lorey, *The U.S.-Mexican Border in the Twentieth Century* (1999).

Cloth ISBN 0-8420-2755-6 Paper ISBN 0-8420-2756-4

Joanne Hershfield and David R. Maciel, eds., *Mexico's Cinema: A Century of Films and Filmmakers* (2000). Cloth ISBN 0-8420-2681-9 Paper ISBN 0-8420-2682-7

Peter V. N. Henderson, *In the Absence of Don Porfirio: Francisco León de la Barra and the Mexican Revolution* (2000). ISBN 0-8420-2774-2

Mark T. Gilderhus, *The Second Century: U.S.-Latin American Relations since 1889* (2000). Cloth ISBN 0-8420-2413-1 Paper ISBN 0-8420-2414-X

Catherine Moses, *Real Life in Castro's Cuba* (2000). Cloth ISBN 0-8420-2836-6 Paper ISBN 0-8420-2837-4

K. Lynn Stoner, ed./comp., with Luis Hipólito Serrano Pérez, *Cuban and Cuban-American Women: An Annotated Bibliography* (2000). ISBN 0-8420-2643-6

Thomas D. Schoonover, *The French in Central America: Culture and Commerce, 1820–1930* (2000). ISBN 0-8420-2792-0

ISBN 0-8420-2755-6